STAR WARS®
EPISODE III
REVENGE OF THE SITH

PRIMA Official Game Guide

Michael Knight

Prima Games
A Division of Random House, Inc.

3000 Lava Ridge Court, Suite 100
Roseville, CA 95661
1-800-733-3000
www.primagames.com

The Prima Games logo is a registered trademark of Random House, Inc., registered in the United States and other countries. Primagames.com is a registered trademark of Random House, Inc., registered in the United States. Prima Games is a division of Random House, Inc.

Product Manager: Mario De Govia
Editorial Supervisor: Christy Seifert
Design & Layout: Derek Hocking, Simon Olney

Acknowledgments
Prima would like to thank: Justin Lambros, Corrine Wong, Matthew Fillbrandt, Tim Moore, Sam Saliba, James Morris, and Michael Blair from LucasArts; and Jeremy Lee from The Collective.

The author would like to thank Christy Seifert and Mario de Govia at Prima. Thanks for the opportunity to do something I love and enjoy.
  I also want to express my love and appreciation to my wife Trisa for her patience and understanding as I labor to meet deadlines. I promise to stop trying to turn out the lights using Jedi Force powers. Hugs to my children, who have to put up with the sound of laser blasts and lightsaber hum at all hours of the day and night.
  Most importantly, I offer my gratitude to my Padawan and five-year-old son Connor, who helped with the multiplayer gameplay, providing me with both a partner and an opponent. Thanks for letting me experiment with different moves and attack combos against you, when what you really wanted to do was fight the duel and beat me (which you did a few times).

ISBN: 0-7615-5164-6
Library of Congress Catalog Card Number: 2005923806
Printed in the United States of America

05 06 07 08 LL 10 9 8 7 6 5 4 3 2 1

Contents

Introduction

The Circle Is Now Complete

Nearly three decades ago, the world was given a new story about the fight between good and evil. Set a long time ago in a galaxy far, far away, *Star Wars*® garnered a following unlike any other movie before or since. While many saw this movie as a beginning, the opening lines of the introduction listed this movie as *Episode IV: A New Hope*. Continuing on with two additional sequels, the original *Star Wars* trilogy left many fans wondering about the obvious trilogy that must tell the story of the Old Republic, the Clone Wars, the destruction of the Jedi, and the creation of the Galactic Empire with its nemesis: the Rebellion. In the last few years, the first two chapters of this pre-story have been told. It is now time for the final chapter, which will link the previous two to the original three.

In the past, reliving the early movies consisted mainly of simulating the battles between the Rebels and the Imperials with plastic action figures, with all motion and sound effects provided by the owners themselves. However, since that time and with the advent of computers and video-game consoles, the action has been heightened and the effects multiplied, until it is almost to the point of controlling the various characters within a movie itself. In *Star Wars*®: **Episode III** *Revenge of the Sith*, you have the opportunity to become a Jedi and fight through many of the battles and climactic duels from the final *Star Wars* movie.

How to Use This Guide

This guide will help you not only survive and complete this game, but also to master it and get more out of the game. To facilitate this, the guide has been organized into three main sections.

The first section covers the game basics. In the "Anakin and Obi-Wan" chapter, you will learn how to control these two main characters as they progress through the story missions. You will also find complete lists of actions, attacks, and combos.

The "Jedi Training" chapter features information and tips on the various moves, Force powers, and actions you can use as a Jedi. It also provides an understanding of how the experience and skill system functions as well as tactics for fighting as a Jedi.

For the information on the other characters in the game, check out the "Allies and Enemies" chapter. Here you get bios on those you fight with and against, as well as how to beat each of your enemies.

The second section of the guide covers the single-player game. These mission chapters provide walkthroughs for the 17 story missions and the 5 bonus missions that you can unlock as you progress through the story missions.

The last section focuses entirely on the multiplayer games. The "Multiplayer Duelists" chapter provides information, tactics, and lists of each duelist's basic actions and special attacks.

In the "Duel Arenas" chapter, you will learn about each of the 14 locations where you can engage in duels against other players. Finally, the "Challenge Mission" chapters offer walkthroughs for all four missions where you and another player can work together to defeat your enemies.

www.lucasarts.com/eps

Anakin and Obi-Wan

Star Wars: **Episode III** *Revenge of the Sith* features a single-player story mode that allows you to play through 17 different missions. During the course of these missions, you will play as either Anakin Skywalker or Obi-Wan Kenobi. Which Jedi you control depends on the mission.

While the two Jedi have many similarities, each has his own strengths and unique attacks. In order to complete the story missions, you must master each Jedi, learning their actions and how best to fight with their own styles.

Anakin Skywalker

Prophesied to be the one to bring balance to the Force, Anakin Skywalker was rescued from a life of slavery on the desert world of Tatooine and brought into the Jedi Order at a relatively late age. Brash and quick-tempered, he learned to calm his anger and master his considerable Force powers under Obi-Wan Kenobi's guidance. Yet all is not well with young Skywalker. His fraternal feelings toward Obi-Wan strain under the weight of resentment and distrust, and a rift with the Jedi Order is forming due to their persecution of his friend and mentor, Chancellor Palpatine. His true destiny has become clouded.

COMBAT CHARTS

Anakin has several different actions, attacks, and combos that he can call upon to defeat his enemies. Following is a list of all the combos available to him. Not all of these are available at the game's beginning. In order to unlock the more advanced attacks, you must earn experience as you progress through the story missions; you can then upgrade Anakin's abilities to use the Force and perform more advanced attacks.

Basic Controls

Name	Xbox	PS2
Run	→	Left analog ⇨
Jump	Ⓐ	✕
Fast slash	Ⓧ	■
Strong slash	Ⓨ	▲
Critical strike	Ⓑ	●
Block	Ⓛ	L1
Saber throw	WHT	L2
Force push/grasp	Ⓡ	R1
Target select	Ⓡ	Right analog
Strafe	Hold Ⓛ+→	Hold L1 + Left analog ⇨
Force stun/lightning		R2
Force heal	Click Ⓛ+Ⓡ	Click left analog + right analog
Force speed	→,→	Left analog ⇨, left analog ⇨

Basic Combos

Name	Xbox	PS2
Standing Rapid Slash Combo	Ⓧ,Ⓧ,Ⓧ	■,■,■
Standing Rapid Back Strike	Ⓧ,Ⓧ,Ⓨ	■,■,▲
Standing Rapid Jung Slash	Ⓧ,Ⓨ,Ⓨ	■,▲,▲
Rapid Slash Combo	→+Ⓧ,Ⓧ,Ⓧ	Left analog ⇨ + ■,■,■
Spinning Jung Ma	→+Ⓧ,Ⓨ,Ⓨ,Ⓨ	Left analog ⇨ + ■,▲,▲,▲
Double Strike Launcher	→+Ⓧ,Ⓧ,Ⓨ,Ⓨ	Left analog ⇨ + ■,■,▲,▲
Double Strike Sai Ma	→+Ⓧ,Ⓧ,Ⓧ,Ⓨ	Left analog ⇨ + ■,■,■,▲
Power Slash Combo	→+Ⓨ,Ⓨ,Ⓨ	Left analog ⇨ + ▲,▲,▲
Power Flurry Combo	→+Ⓨ,Ⓧ,Ⓧ	Left analog ⇨ + ▲,■,■
Power Kick Combo	→+Ⓨ,Ⓨ,Ⓧ	Left analog ⇨ + ▲,▲,■

Saber Locks/Shunts

Name	Xbox	PS2
Initiate Saber Lock	Ⓨ	▲
Saber Lock Struggle	Rapidly press Ⓧ,Ⓨ	Rapidly press ■,▲
Saber Lock Fast Attack	Ⓧ	■
Saber Lock Strong Attack	Ⓨ	▲
Saber Shunt	→+Ⓛ	Left analog ⇨+L1
Saber Trap Shunt	←+Ⓛ	Left analog ⇦+L1
Fast Shunt Attack	Ⓧ	■
Strong Shunt Attack	Ⓨ	▲

Jump Attacks

Name	Xbox	PS2
Rapid Sai Air Combo	Ⓐ,Ⓧ,Ⓧ,Ⓧ	✕,■,■,■
Jumping Roundhouse Kick	Ⓧ,Ⓧ,←+Ⓨ	■,■, left analog ⇦+▲
Flip Kick (at end of combo)	←+Ⓧ	Left analog ⇦+■
Dodge Counter	Ⓛ+Ⓐ+→,Ⓨ	L1+✕+Left analog ⇨,▲
Vault Attack	Ⓐ+Ⓑ	✕+●
Soaring Back Kick	→+Ⓐ,Ⓨ	Left analog ⇨ + ✕,▲

Grapples

Name	Xbox	PS2
Grab Opponent	X+Y	■+▲
Grapple Judo	X+Y,Y	■+▲,▲
Grapple Kick	X+Y,X	■+▲,■
Grapple Throwdown	X+Y,X,X	■+▲,■,■
Grapple Punt	X+Y,Y,Y	■+▲,▲,▲

Dash Attacks

Name	Xbox	PS2
Launcher Slash (at end of combo)	→+Y	Left analog ⇨ + ▲
Critical Sweeping Lunge	→+ hold B	Left analog ⇨ + hold ●
Dashing Uppercut	→,→+X	Left analog ⇨, left analog ⇨+■
Fury Corkscrew	→ + hold X	Left analog ⇨ + hold ■
Dashing Lunge	→,→+Y	Left analog ⇨, left analog ⇨+▲

Area Attacks

Name	Xbox	PS2
Jumping Sai Smash	A,Y	X,▲
Clearing Sweep (at end of combo)	X+Y	■+▲
Fury Whirlwind	→+ hold Y	Left analog ⇨ + hold ▲
Fury Explosion	Hold Y	Hold ▲
Fury Sai Bomb	A +hold Y	X+hold ▲

Critical Attacks

Name	Xbox	PS2
Critical Strike	B	●
Critical Choke Impale	B,B	●,●
Force Impale (close range)	Hold ℝ,B	Hold R1,●
Critical Throwdown	Hold B	Hold ●
Force Stab (long range)	Hold ℝ,B	Hold R1,●

PLAYING AS ANAKIN

As you play through the story missions, you will notice that each Jedi has subtle differences. As they become more experienced, their differences increase as Anakin turns to the dark side of the Force.

Anakin is a more aggressive fighter. Many of his attacks and abilities are meant to maximize damage to the enemy, while at times leaving Anakin open for counterattack. As such, while playing as Anakin, focus on attacking the enemy. Anakin believes that the best defense is an overwhelming offense. The enemy can't hurt you if he is destroyed. Maintain the initiative during a battle by constantly slashing away, never giving the enemy a chance to regroup or mount their own attack against you.

Obi-Wan Kenobi

No Jedi has had a more direct hand in the fate of the galaxy than Obi-Wan Kenobi. His humble and soft-spoken demeanor belies his warrior prowess, and, alongside his friend and former apprentice, Anakin Skywalker, he has led many devastating strikes against the Separatists. Yet no amount of knowledge or experience could have prepared him for the challenge of training the Chosen One. As the Clone Wars threaten to rip the Republic asunder, so, too, are the brotherly bonds between Obi-Wan and Anakin coming apart. Obi-Wan fears for his friend's future—for his very soul—and he's determined not to lose Anakin to the dark side.

COMBAT CHARTS

Here is a complete list of Obi-Wan's actions and attacks. Like Anakin, not all of these are available initially. The more advanced attacks must be unlocked through the expenditure of experience points at the end of each story mission.

Basic Controls

Name	Xbox	PS2
Run	→	Left analog ⇨
Jump	Ⓐ	✕
Fast slash	Ⓧ	■
Strong slash	Ⓨ	▲
Critical strike	Ⓑ	●
Block	Ⓛ	L1
Saber throw	WHT	L2
Force push/grasp	Ⓡ	R1
Target select	Ⓡ	Right analog
Strafe	Hold Ⓛ+→	Hold L1 + Left analog ⇨
Force stun/Jedi Mind Trick	BLK	R2
Force heal	Click Ⓛ+Ⓡ	Click left analog + right analog
Force speed	→,→	Left analog ⇨, left analog ⇨

Basic Combos

Name	Xbox	PS2
Standing Rapid Slash Combo	Ⓧ,Ⓧ,Ⓧ	■,■,■
Standing Sai Slash	Ⓧ,Ⓧ,Ⓨ	■,■,▲
Standing Rapid Sweep	Ⓧ,Ⓨ,Ⓨ	■,▲,▲
Standing Power Slash Combo	Ⓨ,Ⓨ	▲,▲
Rapid Slash Combo	→+Ⓧ,Ⓧ,Ⓧ	Left analog ⇨ + ■,■,■
Slashing Jung Thrust	→+Ⓧ,Ⓨ,Ⓨ,Ⓨ	Left analog ⇨+ ■,▲,▲,▲
Slashing Spin Kick	→+Ⓧ,Ⓧ,Ⓨ,Ⓨ	Left analog ⇨ + ■,■,▲,▲
Power Slash Combo	→+Ⓨ,Ⓨ,Ⓨ	Left analog ⇨+ ▲,▲,▲
Power Flurry Combo	→+Ⓨ,Ⓧ,Ⓧ	Left analog ⇨+ ▲,■,■
Power Sweeping Combo	→+Ⓨ,Ⓨ,Ⓧ	Left analog ⇨+ ▲,▲,■

Saber Locks/Shunts

Name	Xbox	PS2
Initiate Saber Lock	Ⓨ	▲
Saber Lock Struggle	Rapidly press Ⓧ,Ⓨ	Rapidly press ■,▲
Saber Lock Fast Attack	Ⓧ	■
Saber Lock Strong Attack	Ⓨ	▲
Saber Shunt	→+Ⓛ	Left analog ⇨ + L1
Saber Trap Shunt	←+Ⓛ	Left analog ⇨, hold L1,■+▲
Fast Shunt Attack	Ⓧ	■
Strong Shunt Attack	Ⓨ	▲

Jump Attacks

Name	Xbox	PS2
Rapid Sai Air Combo	Ⓐ,Ⓧ,Ⓧ,Ⓧ	✕,■,■,■
Jumping Double Crescent	Ⓧ,Ⓧ,→+Ⓨ	■,■, left analog ⇨+▲
Flip Kick (at end of combo)	←+Ⓧ	Left analog ⇦+■
Dodge Counter	Ⓛ+Ⓐ+→,Ⓨ	L1+✕+ Left analog ⇨, ▲
Vault Attack	Ⓐ+Ⓑ	✕+●
Soaring Back Kick	→+Ⓐ,Ⓨ	Left analog ⇨ + ✕,Ⓨ

Grapples

Name	Xbox	PS2
Grab Opponent	Ⓧ+Ⓨ	■+▲
Grapple Punch	Ⓧ+Ⓨ,Ⓨ	■+▲,▲
Grapple Kick	Ⓧ+Ⓨ,Ⓧ	■+▲,■
Grapple Throwdown	Ⓧ+Ⓨ,Ⓧ,Ⓧ	■+▲,■,■
Grapple Judo	Ⓧ+Ⓨ,Ⓨ,Ⓨ	■+▲,▲,▲

Dash Attacks

Name	Xbox	PS2
Launcher Slash (at end of combo)	→+Ⓨ	Left analog ⇨ +▲
Critical Sweeping Lunge	→ + hold Ⓑ	Left analog ⇨+ hold ●
Dashing Uppercut	→,→+Ⓧ	Left analog ⇨, left analog ⇨+■
Focus Lunge Strike	Hold →+Ⓧ	Hold Left analog ⇨+ ■
Dashing Lunge	→,→+Ⓨ	Left analog ⇨, left analog ⇨ + ▲

Area Attacks

Name	Xbox	PS2
Jumping Sai Smash	Ⓐ,Ⓨ	✕,▲
Palm Shock (at end of combo)	Ⓧ+Ⓨ	■+▲
Focus Shockwave	Hold →+Ⓨ	Hold Left analog ⇨ + ▲
Focus Slash Combo	Hold Ⓨ	Hold ▲
Focus Sai Bomb	Ⓐ +hold Ⓨ	✕ +hold ▲

Critical Attacks

Name	Xbox	PS2
Critical Strike	Ⓑ	●
Critical Arm Slice	Ⓑ,Ⓑ	●,●
Saber Impale (close range)	Hold Ⓡ,Ⓑ	Hold R1,●
Critical Sweeping Lunge	Hold Ⓑ	Hold ●
Neck Strike (long range)	Hold Ⓡ,Ⓑ	Hold R1,●

PLAYING AS OBI-WAN

While Anakin is an aggressive fighter, Obi-Wan is a bit more defensive. That does not mean he cannot dish out damage like Anakin. Instead, Obi-Wan is a Jedi Master whose style epitomizes mastery in classical Jedi training. Focused, well-balanced, and resilient, Obi-Wan is better at blocking and waiting for the right moment to strike. Use his Force powers, such as Force stun to momentarily stop an enemy from doing anything, thus allowing you to get in several hits without your target being able to block you. Later on, Obi-Wan can even use the Jedi Mind Trick to get organics (non-droids) to fight on his side rather than against him for a limited amount of time. As the story missions progress and as Anakin and Obi-Wan's paths begin to diverge, it is important that you play each Jedi according to their strengths in order to maximize the effectiveness of their abilities and attacks.

Jedi Training

You must master the ways of the Jedi if you wish to survive.

In this game, you take on the role of a Jedi and must fight like a Jedi. Unlike other games where you may have a dozen or more weapons you can use to achieve victory, in this game you use a single weapon—the lightsaber. Use this Jedi tool for attacking, defending, and even for cutting through metal to access locked areas.

There are four main categories of things you can do as a Jedi: basic actions, attack combos, Force powers, and advanced moves and actions. In order to improve your Force powers and unlock advanced moves and actions, you must earn experience points during the story missions. After you learn all of this, you will be ready to fight as a Jedi.

NOTE

All actions and attacks have unique button presses to activate them. Because this guide covers both the Xbox and PS2 versions of the game, this chapter refers to what buttons do as opposed to actual button designations on the controller. See the previous section, "Anakin and Obi-Wan," for complete button charts of these actions and attacks.

Basic Actions

As with most learning, it is important to start with the basics. After you master these, then you can move on to other things. This is true for playing as a Jedi. Basic actions are performed by a single button press or with the analog stick. There are two main types of basic actions—movement and attacks.

MOVEMENT

To move around in the game, use the left analog stick. A little pressure on this stick causes your character to walk; pushing it all the way orders your character to run in that direction. Your Jedi automatically turns in the direction you indicate.

To get over obstacles or over an enemy, press the Jump button to jump into the air. Combine this with moving the analog stick to cause your Jedi to jump in the indicated direction.

ATTACKS

A quick slash is a good way to get in a quick hit and is a good start for additional attacks

To survive and complete your missions, you must be able to attack. The main attack method is slashing with your lightsaber. You can choose from a quick slash or a strong slash. The quick slash does not cause as much damage as a strong slash. However, the latter is more likely to be blocked or deflected by the enemy. In addition, you can make a critical strike. Each of these three attacks is controlled by a unique button on your controller. You can also make some attacks using the Force, which are discussed in the following "Force Powers" section.

While attacking is important, you must also be able to defend yourself. The Block button is very important—especially while dueling against another Jedi. Hold down this button to block an enemy lightsaber or other melee weapon and to repel weak blaster fire. If you move while pressing this button, you will strafe. This means that instead of your Jedi turning in the direction of the motion, he will continue facing the closest enemy. This is important when fighting in close, since your block only affects attacks made against you from the front. Pressing the Jump button while blocking and moving causes your Jedi to stop blocking and make a short hop in the desired direction, all the while keeping his lightsaber up and ready to block.

Attack Combos

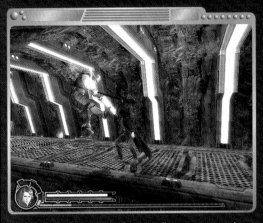

Combine a series of attacks to really cause some damage to your enemies.

String together a series of attacks to create "combos." Most combos consist of a series of two or three attack buttons pressed in a certain order. Others may combine movement or even a jump with an attack to make your Jedi perform various attacks you cannot perform with a single button press. There are many different combos, and the same combination of buttons may yield different attacks depending on the Jedi.

Force Powers

Jedi can use the Force to attack or accomplish different actions. There are three buttons that deal with the Force. Most of these require a target. Move the right analog stick to select targets for your Force actions. Targets have a blue glow, so you know which target you are choosing.

FORCE PUSH AND FORCE GRASP

The Force Push/Grasp button quickly pushes a target away from you, usually causing some damage. Hold down this button to lift your target. Then you can move the left analog stick to throw the target in the corresponding direction. Use this move to throw objects at enemies or to throw enemies themselves.

FORCE STUN, FORCE LIGHTNING, AND JEDI MIND TRICK

Stunning powerful droids can let you attack them for a short period of time while they can't block.

The second Force action is the Force stun. When you press this button, your Jedi uses the Force to stun the targeted droid or enemy. Later in the game, when you press this button, Anakin attacks with Force lightning, which damages the target, and Obi-Wan can Jedi Mind Trick targeted clones into fighting for him rather than against him.

SABER THROW

Another Force action is the saber throw. Press this button to make the Jedi throw his lightsaber at the target. The longer you hold down the button, the farther the lightsaber travels (up to its maximum distance). Increase this distance by upgrading this Force power.

FORCE DEFLECT

Force deflect can be a great way to prevent getting killed by turrets.

Sometimes you face an enemy with a lot of firepower. It could be a powerful droid or a turret. You can use the Force to deflect the shots from these enemies back at them—using their own firepower to destroy them. To perform this action, hold down the Block button and move the right analog stick in a circle. Your Jedi will swing his lightsaber in a circular motion, deflecting all shots 180 degrees in front of your character back at the enemy.

FORCE HEAL

You can also use the Force to heal yourself. Press down on both analog sticks simultaneously and your Jedi uses his Force power to restore his health. This is useful during a long fight. However, you are vulnerable while Force healing. During the single-player missions, you can use experience points to upgrade your Force heal ability.

FORCE SPEED

Force speed quickly gets you where you need to go. It also makes it very difficult for enemies to hit you while moving so fast.

The final Force power is Force speed. Tap the left analog stick twice in a direction for a short burst of speed. Combining Force speed with attack combos to create some powerful attacks.

MISSION-REQUIRED FORCE ACTIONS

In single-player mode, you may also be required to use the Force to continue to the next area. In those cases, move to the spot indicated by a glowing circle on the ground and press the button listed on the screen. Force jump allows you to jump to locations otherwise not accessible, and Force focus often involves moving a heavy obstacle using the Force.

Advanced Moves and Actions

GRAPPLES

Grapples are a good way to get in an attack on an opponent who constantly blocks your slashes and attack combos. Think of grapples as a changeup attack.

Grapples are attacks where you grab your enemies and then either throw, kick, or punch them. They require you to be adjacent to your target. If you are ever caught in a grapple, press the Quick and Strong Slash buttons simultaneously at the grapple's beginning to break out of it. These buttons also help you break out of a stun or help you avoid being attacked while lying on the ground.

UNIVERSAL LAUNCHER AND AIR TECH ESCAPE

As the third part of a three-button combo, move toward your opponent and press the Strong Slash button. This causes your opponent to go flying into the air. Jump up after them to make a follow-up attack. On the other hand, if you are the one being launched, press the Jump button while in the air to perform an Air Tech Escape and avoid the follow-up attack.

SHUNTS AND SABER LOCKS

When fighting against another Jedi or opponent with a lightsaber, you can parry or shunt a lightsaber strike by pressing the Block button while moving away from your opponent. Press either the Quick or Strong Slash button for a follow-up attack. If your opponent shunts your attack, press one of the Slash buttons quickly. If you chose the same one as your opponent's follow-up attack, you escape the attack. If you want to perform a shunt that can't be countered, press the two Slash buttons simultaneously while blocking, just before your opponent hits you. This is called a Trap Shunt.

Whenever two Jedi attack with a strong slash at the same time, their lightsabers lock together. When this happens, rapidly press the Quick and Strong Slash buttons simultaneously to push your opponent back and get in a free attack.

Experience and Skills

Your experience is tallied at the end of each mission. You then get to spend it on upgrading your powers and attacks.

During the story missions, you earn experience points when you defeat an enemy. The amount of points you receive depends on your skill meter.

Skill accumulates as you attack enemies. Even blocked attacks receive some skill, but at a lower rate than for hits. Your skill meter actually decreases as you take hits, block attacks, or don't attack anything for a period of time. Therefore, it is beneficial to stay on the offensive as much as possible.

Whenever an enemy is defeated, you receive a combat rating for the kill. If your skill level is low, you receive a Fair rating and the appropriate experience points. If you have a medium skill level, then you get a Good rating with a 150 percent bonus to the experience points earned. A high skill level provides an Impressive rating with a 200 percent experience bonus. Finally, if you can completely fill the skill meter, you get a Masterful rating with a 300 percent bonus for a limited amount of time. In addition, each attack during this Masterful period causes increased damage, and enemies cannot block your attacks.

At the mission's end, your total experience points earned are tallied. You can then use these points to upgrade your Force powers and/or to unlock new attack combos. The experience points earned during a mission are only applied to the Jedi you controlled. Therefore, during the course of the story missions, you upgrade both Anakin and Obi-Wan separately.

SECRETS

Find secrets in most of the story missions.

Most story missions contain secrets. In the initial overview for the mission, you are informed of how many secrets are contained in the mission. Secrets are revealed in several ways. Some may require you to destroy one or more containers, power cables, or other objects. Find others by moving through an area or even by standing in one place for a certain amount of time. If you don't find all of the secrets in a mission, you can replay it to find those you missed. However, when replaying a mission, secrets you already discovered no longer exist.

There are three types of secrets—health surge, Force surge, and saber crystal.

Health Surge
This secret increases the maximum capacity of your health meter and fills it completely.

Force Surge
Force surge increases your maximum Force power and fills the meter.

Saber Crystal
Saber crystal fills your skill meter, giving you the Masterful rating for any enemies defeated for a limited amount of time. Whenever you find this, quickly rush into battle to maximize your experience points earned for the mission.

Fighting as a Jedi

The great number of different actions and attacks you can do can be quite overwhelming at the start. However, not all of the combos and advanced attacks are available until later in the game, when you have earned enough experience points to upgrade, so focus on the actions and attacks you begin with, and by the time you master them, others will be added.

Remember that you can use the Force during combat. A common mistake young Padawans or Jedi in training make is to focus primarily on their lightsaber skills. Slashing away at a blocking opponent often gets you nowhere. However, a quick Force push or throw can break a block, allowing you to get in some hits. Throwing an object at your opponent has the same result, plus it causes damage from the impact and possible explosion. When facing several enemies, try throwing an enemy at other enemies to damage both at the same time. Your Force powers can also allow you to attack or deal with enemies out of your range by throwing your lightsaber at a target or by pulling a distant enemy off a ledge. There is rarely a single solution to a challenge, and over time you will develop your own fighting style. New enemies may require new tactics in order to defeat them. Try different things until you find something that works.

Allies and Enemies

In addition to the two Jedi you play as, there are a host of other characters you interact with throughout the single-player story missions. Some of these characters are allies who fight alongside you, but most of them fight against you. There are even some who can be an ally during one mission and an enemy later.

It is important for you to know your allies and how they can help—and even more importantly, know the strengths and weaknesses of your enemies. Therefore, study the various characters you will encounter.

Republic Characters

As the Separatists began to attack systems within the Republic, the main peacekeeper for thousands of years—the Jedi—have been forced into the role of defenders and soldiers. Overwhelmed and outnumbered by their enemies, the Republic turns to clones to form the Grand Army; thus begins the Clone Wars that will end with the destruction of the Republic and the birth of the Galactic Empire.

MACE WINDU

A respected senior member of the Jedi Council, Mace Windu is a diplomat skilled in the art of aggressive negotiations. His proficiency with a lightsaber is matched only by his ability to resolve a conflict without igniting said blade. Nowhere will you find a Jedi with a more commanding presence. His words carry great weight with the Galactic Senate, yet he finds himself increasingly at odds with the political body he's vowed to protect, enforcing his belief that a Sith Lord is manipulating events and bringing strife to the Republic. Windu has devoted himself to uncovering this shadowy menace's true identity.

Anakin will fight a duel against Mace Windu about halfway through the story missions. Windu's fighting style is powerful and efficient. Every move and attack focuses on a purpose—to strike at the enemy. Therefore, you will not see a lot of jumping and wide slashing actions. Because of this, Windu can be tough to hit. You must constantly block since each hit by Windu causes more damage than you inflict on him. Dodge his grapple attacks and wait for an opening. In many cases, you must use Force powers to create an opening so you can defeat this Jedi Master.

www.lucasarts.com/eps

CIN DRALLIG

An esteemed Jedi Master and a swordsman of nearly unparalleled skills, Cin Drallig represents the Jedi Order's tenets in their purest form. Making his home deep within the Jedi Temple, he has given himself over completely to the will of the living Force, dedicating his life to teaching Jedi Padawans the Order's values and beliefs and training them in the most precise lightsaber arts. Patient, focused, and directed, Cin Drallig is a most formidable opponent to anyone who would dare stand against the Jedi.

Anakin must duel against Cin Drallig during his final mission in the Jedi Temple. As an instructor at the Jedi Temple, Drallig is a master with the lightsaber and can perform many different and powerful attacks. While his dueling style is focused and deliberate, he can also be very energetic. Some of his attacks are so fast that he appears as a blur, slashing at his opponent so quickly that there is no chance for blocking. When fighting against Cin Drallig, use Force powers to break up his blocks or make your own attack at the very end of one of his combos, when he is susceptible to your own combos. Also, stay at a distance while his Force meter is maxed out, or you may be on the receiving end of his fast special attacks.

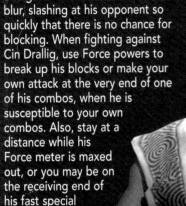

SERRA KETO

Not all of legendary Jedi Master Cin Drallig's students share his calmness of mind and spirit. Throughout her Padawan training, Serra's headstrong and defiant ways confounded her Jedi Masters, nearly leading to her expulsion from the Jedi Order on more than one occasion. Cin Drallig saw through Serra's contentiousness and envisioned the great Jedi she could potentially become. Under his tutelage, Serra's understanding of the Force grows, and her lightsaber skills blossom, inspiring a strong bond of devotion between student and Master. Though her rebelliousness eventually subsided, Serra's still prone to moments of restlessness and impatience. While her speed in duels approaches that of her master, Cin Drallig, Serra is also very dynamic and acrobatic.

Many of her attacks feature spins, jumps, and other moves as a part of a combo of slashes. Even her signature grapple attack, which ends with a launching kick, would be considered artistic if it didn't hurt her opponents so much. While Serra lacks the power of a Jedi Master, her use of dual lightsabers makes up for this in damage inflicted and wide angle of attack. In fact, if you are anywhere near Serra, she can hit you with her spinning slashes. The key to defeating Serra is to block her spinning attacks and get her off balance by throwing objects at her or throwing her around. Whenever her guard is down, rush in for fast and powerful attacks. While she is blocking, use Force-powered combos that cannot be blocked. It is also important to keep moving and be ready to jump out of the way of her dash attacks.

YODA

There are few Jedi as long-lived and farsighted as Master Yoda. Throughout his 900 years, he's trained many Jedi and has watched the rise, fall, and resolution of many galaxy-spanning political crises. Yet none have troubled him as deeply as have the Clone Wars and the apparent return of the Sith. Fearing the worst—that the Jedi Order is unraveling and that his own connection to the Force is wavering—Yoda presses to find the Sith Lord who is orchestrating the Republic-Separatist conflict, knowing that if he fails, the entire galaxy will be lost in darkness.

Yoda fights alongside you during one of the missions. In addition, you can also take control of the small yet powerful Jedi in a bonus mission that is unlocked during the course of the story missions. Yoda's fighting style features constant motion as the Jedi leaps and flies through the air to attack much larger enemies.

JEDI KNIGHT

Sworn to uphold peace and justice throughout the galaxy, the Jedi Knights have served the Republic for generations. Formidable warriors in their own right, the Jedi prefer to resolve conflict through diplomacy and nonviolent means. Only when that fails do they draw their lightsabers and engage in direct physical action, often with swift and decisive results. As the Clone Wars have worn on, the Jedi have found themselves fulfilling the roles of generals of the Republic's armies, while their connection to the Force has become obscured.

Anakin faces Jedi Knights while in the Jedi Temple. They are able to block some of your slashes, so it takes some effort to defeat them. Often a good combo or two breaks through their blocks, allowing you to eliminate these Jedi and move on to other opposition.

JEDI PADAWAN

When a person is brought into the Jedi Order and taught the ways of the living Force, the first rank they achieve is that of Padawan. Working first in groups with other similarly skilled apprentices and later paired with an individual Jedi Knight or Master, the Padawans' abilities are ever growing and are not to be underestimated. Though they are only just learning the extent of their burgeoning powers, the Padawans are a formidable force, representing the hope and future of the Jedi Order.

Jedi Padawans don't have a chance against Anakin. However, they bravely defend the Temple and can be a threat since they usually are found in groups. A single combo that ends with a critical strike will usually take care of these weak Jedi. If there are other more powerful enemies, ignore the Padawans and go after the tougher Jedi who can cause more damage. Then return to finish off the Padawans.

JEDI SNIPER

Jedi Snipers also act as defenders of the Jedi Temple, though rather than relying on the Jedi Brutes' raw physical strength to dispose of their assailants, the Jedi Snipers have perfected the art of long-range lightsaber attacks. So attuned to the Force are they, the snipers have achieved an almost symbiotic relationship with their own weapons, enabling them to throw and control their lightsabers over long distances with devastating precision.

With the exception of Jedi Masters, Jedi Snipers are the only Jedi who throw their lightsabers. In fact, that is their main type of attack. Found in the Jedi Temple, they will usually remain at a distance from you and will concentrate on their ranged attack. Since this can be damaging, Jedi Snipers should take precedence over other Jedi attackers. Get in close to attack with a combo and you will have little trouble defeating them since their melee skills are not very good. Just watch out for the flying lightsabers as you approach them.

JEDI BRUTE

Protectors of the Jedi Temple, the Jedi Brutes are larger and more tactically aggressive than the average Jedi. Selected for their imposing physical nature, the Brutes are instructed from a young age in the Order's more direct and hands-on fighting styles. While their imposing mass alone is enough to dissuade those who would seek to degrade the Jedi Temple, their fearsome appearance belies their peaceful and intelligent nature. Unprovoked, the Brutes are kind and gentle. When the Jedi in the Temple are threatened, however, you won't find a more ferocious warrior.

Jedi Brutes are very tough opponents. In fact, any engagement against them is almost a duel in itself. Armed with a double-bladed lightsaber, Jedi Brutes can block most standard combos and can block all but the most powerful Force lightning and push attacks. Your best bet is to use Force grasp to pick them up and throw them or at least to break their block and get in a few hits of your own. Force-based combos are usually your best bet since they can break through a block. Follow them up with combos 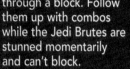 while the Jedi Brutes are stunned momentarily and can't block.

COMMANDER CODY

Commander Cody is one of the first to emerge from an experimental training program designed to encourage more cognitive thinking among the rank-and-file clone troopers. Proving time and again to be a brilliant strategist and shrewd tactician on the battlefield, Cody has served many missions alongside Jedi Knight Obi-Wan Kenobi; over time, the two men have become fast friends. Troopers that serve under Cody often develop unwavering loyalty toward the commander and are known to put their own lives on the line to protect him. He is one of the Republic's bravest and most valuable allies.

Commander Cody brings in reinforcements for Obi-Wan on Utapau and later sends in his troopers to attack his former Jedi general. Cody appears only in the cutscenes and never actually fights with or against you during the missions.

CLONE TROOPER

The clone troopers are bred for one purpose only—to carry out the will of the Republic. Commissioned by a mysterious member of the Jedi Order and based on a genetic template provided by famed Mandalorian bounty hunter Jango Fett, the clone troopers were created to quell the growing Separatist uprising, a task they pursue with aggression and efficiency. Trained in various weapons and combat skills, the clone troopers never question their role in the war or think outside of their preprogrammed parameters, making them an invaluable component of the Jedi and Republic forces.

You have the opportunity to both fight alongside and against clone troopers. Their main weapon is the blaster rifle. As such, they will try to attack at range. However, if an enemy gets in close, they can use the butt of their rifle for a melee attack. You will need a few lightsaber slashes to defeat clone troopers. Fast slashes usually work best since they will probably hit more than one trooper as they often attack in groups. Obi-Wan can use the Jedi Mind Trick on clone troopers, temporarily causing them to fight for the Jedi rather than against him.

CLONE HEAVY GUNNER

A variation on the standard clone trooper, the heavy gunners carry the most powerful weapons wielded by a single Republic unit. Primarily intended for use against tanks and other armored vehicles, they've also proven quite capable against the Separatists' air units. The clone heavy gunners specialize in quick, devastating strikes and deadly bombardments. Opponents are often advised to take cover at the first sight of a heavy gunner, though this strategy's effectiveness has yet to be proven.

Carrying a weapon more suited to an antiarmor role, clone heavy gunners are a major threat during a mission. A single hit from their weapon can cause a lot of damage and also knocks you down, allowing other enemies to attack you. As a result, always keep your eyes open for clone heavy gunners and make them your priority targets, neutralizing them before they can hurt you.

CLONE BLAZE TROOPER

The clone blaze troopers are engineered for the Clone War's harshest and most unforgiving conditions. Equipped with heavy and nearly impenetrable armor and carrying massive flamethrowers capable of melting most metals, the blaze troopers are also outfitted with personal jet-propulsion gear and trained in forms of aerial combat. Often sent ahead of the clone army's forces, blaze troopers can also clear battlefield wreckage and environmental obstructions. After they're released, the blaze troopers burn through enemies and obstacles with unstoppable force.

Flying around the battle area, blaze troopers can quickly approach and attack you. They like to get in close to use their flamethrower and grapple. Because of their heavy armor, these troopers can take a lot of damage and can block some of your slashes. Their weight also makes them difficult to Force push or grasp. The best way to defeat blaze troopers is through a series of combos. Since they can attack in groups, quick slashes and Force-powered combos work best, allowing you to hit several nearby enemies at once.

CLONE ASSASSIN

The clone assassins are of the same genetic family as the ARC (Advanced Recon Commandos) troopers and are considered some of the most elite and deadly in the entire Republic army. Allowed more mental freedom than the average clone trooper and being closer in thinking and attitude to their progenitor Jango Fett, the clone assassins are designed to work in small groups, performing special infiltration and assassination operations. Trained in close-quarters hand-to-hand combat, the clone assassins are famed for their stealth and precision. If you see one coming, it's already too late.

Clone assassins are extremely tough enemies. With their speed, they can dodge attacks so quickly that they appear as a blur. Through intense training in the arts of Tera Kasi, the clone assassins' senses have become tuned so accurately that they are known to even dodge the grip of Force powers. Armed with two vibroblades that sweep out into position from arm-mounted sheaths, their attacks are equally fast. The best way to defeat these enemies (that usually come at you in groups) is by fast slash combos, which focus on speed rather than power, and Force-powered area attacks. Force push can also work well, pushing groups of clone assassins back and causing some damage in the process.

Separatist Characters

Members of the Confederacy of Independent Systems, the Separatists desire to break away from the Republic and take as many worlds as possible with them. The main fighting force of the Separatists are droids that can be mass produced and shipped wherever they are needed.

COUNT DOOKU

Before embracing the dark side of the Force and allying himself with the Sith, Count Dooku was once a Jedi of much esteem, even having the privilege of training directly under Master Yoda. Yet with all the promise of greatness he possessed, he could no longer stand by and watch the Republic sink under what he saw as irreversible corruption. Renouncing his Jedi commission, Dooku vanished for several years, reemerging again as the mastermind behind the Confederacy of Independent Systems and as a secret servant of Darth Sidious. A man of elegance and charm, Dooku's most dangerous weapon is his intoxicating personality.

Count Dooku is the first duel you must fight in the story missions. As such, he is the first opponent who fights in a similar way as you. In order to survive the fight with Dooku, you must block his attacks and then get in your own attacks. Dooku's style reflects the short slashes and thrusts common to fencing rather than the Jedi's wide, spinning slashes. As such, his attacks are focused and deliberate. Count Dooku also uses the Force for grasping and throwing and for special, unique attacks. Fight defensively and use your own Force powers to break up his blocks and attacks.

GENERAL GRIEVOUS

A hideous amalgam of cutting-edge Separatist technology and the broken body of a once-proud Kaleesh warrior, General Grievous stormed the Confederacy ranks, quickly becoming leader of the droid armies, second only to Count Dooku. Unrelentingly cruel and unbound by conscience or morals, Grievous hunts Jedi for sport and collects his victim's lightsabers, often keeping his most prized trophies within his cloak. It was Grievous who masterminded the assault on Coruscant and the kidnapping of the chancellor, and nothing would please him more than to add Obi-Wan Kenobi and Anakin Skywalker's blades to his growing collection.

General Grievous, while not a Jedi, fights with two lightsabers. At times, he can pull out two additional lightsabers for a total of four. However, this can only be done for a limited amount of time. Obi-Wan faces General Grievous in a duel on Utapau. The cyborg has some very powerful attacks, including a dash attack that requires a charge-up. When you see Grievous crouch down, get ready to jump to one side or the other to avoid this fast and damaging attack. Lacking Force powers, Grievous can still attack you at range with his blaster. Therefore, no matter where you are when fighting him, you must be ready to dodge or block. Since Grievous is good at blocking, use Force powers to grasp and hold him long enough to get in a combo attack. Saber throws and grapples can also work well against this opponent.

GRIEVOUS BODYGUARD

Grievous' personal bodyguards are each built to the general's very strict specifications. Fiendishly shrewd, the bodyguards often work in tandem, linking their attacks in pairs and breaking their enemies down piece by piece, dealing tremendous damage with their electrostaff weapons. Thoroughly unrelenting, bodyguard droids pursue their targets even after they've been dismembered and seemingly defeated. They will attach their broken frames onto their enemy's bodies and dispatch themselves with fiery explosions.

These are some of the toughest, nonduel opponents you must face during the story missions. In fact, fighting them is essentially a miniduel in itself since they can block your lightsaber with their electrostaffs. A good tactic is to Force grasp them up into the air and then hit them with a combo before they can recover and block. In fact, Force grasp and push can keep them back from you and cause damage. While the Grievous bodyguards can't grapple, you can grapple them, allowing you to get in an attack without worrying about them blocking you. As with other duels, always keep your lightsaber up to block their fast blows or you will take some serious damage, since one hit is usually followed by several more in quick combo attacks.

BATTLE DROIDS

Battle droids are the mechanized spine of the Separatist military. Though not as sturdy or fearsome as their superiorly modified droid counterparts, what the standard battle droid lacks in armament or weaponry it makes up for in tenacity and sheer force of numbers. Single-minded to a fault and unable to formulate alternate strategies, battle droids will doggedly pursue a target until it's been annihilated—or until the droids themselves have been blasted to pieces.

Armed with a droid blaster rifle, battle droids will attack at range and often in groups. The weakest enemy you face, a single slash or even a Force push will often destroy them. When fighting them, use quick slashes that can hit more than one. When facing other types of enemies, battle droids should be last on your priority list. However, if you move near them, eliminate them with a slash while they are in range. You can also Force grasp battle droids and throw them at other enemies, taking care of two droids with one attack.

www.lucasarts.com/eps

SUPER BATTLE DROIDS

Seeing the flaws in the standard battle droid's small frames and limited thought processors, Separatist engineers developed a more aggressive and heavily armored version—the super battle droid. Carrying built-in, wrist-fired laser cannons encased in a thick steel shell and being completely fearless, the super battle droid is quickly becoming the favored unit of the Separatist infantry.

These droids are much tougher than the battle droids. In addition to heavier firepower with a higher rate of fire, the super battle droids are also armored, allowing them to take more damage. It takes at least a three-slash combo and possibly a few more slashes to defeat these enemies. During the early missions, they are your greatest threat. However, even later when you go up against more powerful enemies, the super battle droid's blaster fire makes it a target worthy of your attention. In fact, you should usually go after the super battle droids to stop their ranged attacks, then return to fight other enemies.

DESTROYER DROIDS (DROIDEKA)

While most battle droids are designed to perform various functions on the battlefield, the destroyer droid isn't concerned with piloting speeders or operating scanners. It exists only to blast its targets to oblivion from close range. Protected by a personal deflector shield generator and armed with a pair of tandem-firing, heavy blaster cannons, the destroyer droid is a most fearsome and deadly enemy. Many a Republic soldier has fallen under its guns.

These powerful droids can be initially terrifying until you understand how best to defeat them. Their blaster cannons can cause a lot of damage in a short amount of time. To make it even worse, the destroyer droid's shields can even deflect your lightsaber. They key is to get them to drop their shields. While in motion and shortly after stopping, you have an opportunity to strike them before they can raise their shields. With little armor, a couple slashes does the trick. However, after their shields are raised, you have two choices: First, use Force stun or lightning to stun the destroyers and get them to lower their shields, allowing you to follow up with a slashing attack. The other option is to Force deflect their blaster fire. Since their fire is phased to pass through their shields to attack you, it can also be deflected right back through the shields to damage and eliminate the droid as well.

GRAPPLE DROIDS

Based on the super battle droid model, the grapple droid was designed specifically for the Separatists' siege on Coruscant. General Grievous himself personally oversaw its modifications. Bigger and profoundly more vicious than its predecessors, the grapple droid is equipped with a pair of electrically charged, industrial pinchers, which it uses to crush the life from its enemies. The grapple droid excels at close-quarters combat, and its embrace is quite deadly.

When you first face grapple droids, you may think them nearly indestructible. Their arms can block your lightsaber, and their grapple and slashing attacks can cause a lot of damage. Use Force powers or attacks to get them to drop their attacks. When they go in for a grapple attack, break the grapple and go into an attack combo before the droid can block. Usually you can slice off an arm with a good attack, which makes it harder for the grapple droid to attack or block you and allows you to move in for a finishing attack. Grapple droids take many hits to destroy; this is actually good because it really builds up your skill meter and provides more experience points for upgrading at the mission's end.

AIR BATTLE DROIDS

Air battle droids are the upgraded flying version of the standard battle droid. Unlike the ground units, the fliers are equipped with a short blade, an arm-mounted blaster, and a shield that can block lightsaber attacks. They are effective up close in melee combat. After they land and take up a fighting stance, air battle droids activate an arm shield that allows them to block lightsaber attacks.

When fighting these enemies, hit them while they are still flying. They have no shields activated while airborne and can be eliminated with a couple slashes of the lightsaber. When they are on the ground, with their shields ready, use Force grasp or push to get them to lower their shield, then slash away.

BUZZ DROIDS

Alone, the insectlike buzz droid isn't much of a threat. In large swarms, however, they can overwhelm and dismantle enemy machinery like no other. Deployed at the Battle of Coruscant, these diminutive automatons proved to be a surprising threat to the Republic's fleet. Wielding an assortment of cutting tools and metal-sheering blades, protected by a miniature shield generator, and working in often over-whelming numbers, the buzz droid specializes in quick technological destruction.

These small droids are more of a nuisance than a real threat. However, since they usually attack in groups, their damage can add up. They are easy to destroy with a single slash as they are rolling about on the ground. However, after they open up and deploy, watch out because they will jump and target your head. Keep slashing to eliminate these pests before they can hit you.

CRAB DROIDS

Few droids are as terrifying as the enormous crab droid. Large enough to directly attack and dismantle most Republic tanks and gunships, the crab droid uses its many powerful limbs to pound enemy craft and soldiers to scrap. Despite its speed and surprising maneuverability, the crab droid has a fatal factory defect—its delicate neural-net sensors can be exposed and destroyed through an access port on the droid's back. Separatist engineers are aware of this flaw but are unconcerned, as climbing on the back of a crab droid to deactivate it would take considerable, nearly inhuman, skill.

The Crab Droid has two main attacks—ranged and melee. It can fire its lasers in quick blasts or a continuous stream. Jump out of the way when you see the lasers charging up. If you are close, the crab droid can also perform a charging attack where it rushes toward you and attempts to smash you with its claw legs. Jump back or out of the way when you see this happen. There is only one way to defeat a crab droid—grapple. Approach the droid from the front, after it fires and before it can hit you with its legs. Grapple near the head to jump onto the crab droid's back. Once there, slash away until you get bucked off. Repeat the tactic until the droid is destroyed.

NEIMOIDIAN GUARD

Because the planet Neimoidia's standing army consists entirely of droids that can be deactivated at a central control point, the Neimoidian leaders often turn to mercenaries and convicts for more reliable personal protection. Guards are usually found trolling Neimoidia's prison systems, as guard commanders search for the meanest and most hardened of criminals to recruit into their ranks, offering candidates amnesty or commuted sentences in exchange for protecting the Neimoidian delegation from would-be assassins. It's brutal work with a high fatality rate, and only the most savage live to see any form of retirement.

Armed with a stun prod, Neimoidian guards are fairly weak against a lightsaber. However, since they usually attack in groups, missing one of them with a slash usually means you get stunned. Once stunned, they will keep attacking, making it difficult to break away and block their attacks. When you see a group coming at you, use Force grasp to throw one at the others or use Force push to knock them down. If you can use the Force to whittle a group down to one or two, the fight is much easier.

NEIMOIDIAN BRUTE GUARD

The most unpredictable and barbarous members of the Neimoidian guards are enrolled, often against their will, in the brute program wherein they undergo several extreme genetic enhancements. The results are a physically larger, more furious and unstable combatant, prone to berserker-like outbursts and incidents of violence against their fellow guards. For this reason, the Neimoidian brute guards are often kept in stasis and used only when situations are most critical.

These enemies are tough. Neimoidian brute guards are able to block your lightsaber with their battle axe, making standard combos ineffective. Instead, use Force-powered attacks. While on Mustafar, an even quicker way to defeat them is to Force grasp them and throw them off walkways and platforms into the ever-present magma below. If you can't do that, just throw them toward you and slash away while they are midair.

NEIMOIDIAN SNIPER

Neimoidian snipers are specially trained in the use of long-range tactics and weaponry and have quickly earned the reputation of being the Confederacy's most precise and deadly shooters. Working closely with the various Neimoidian guard factions, the snipers lie in silent wait—for sometimes days at a time—for their marks to be herded toward them. Once the snipers have their targets in their crosshairs, death is immediate and without warning.

Armed with a long rifle, Neimoidian snipers can be easily defeated with a combo attack while in close. However, the snipers rarely let you get that close since they are often located at positions where you cannot reach them—at least physically (you can reach them with the Force). Since their shots are damaging, it is important to deal with them as soon as you see them. Use Force grasp to target them and then either throw them off their platform or toward you where a combo attack finishes them off.

Mission 1: Rescue over Coruscant

Briefing

Jedi: Anakin Skywalker

Location: Separatist Cruiser

Secrets: 3

Anakin Skywalker returns from the Outer Rim to thwart General Grievous' kidnapping plot. Together with Obi-Wan Kenobi, the two Jedi raid the Separatist flagship to locate and retrieve Chancellor Palpatine.

Objective
- Escape the Cruiser hangar

Walkthrough

Anakin and Obi-Wan crash-land their fighters into the hangar of the Separatist cruiser. As soon as you have control of Anakin, move to the right and begin engaging the battle droids. Since they are easy to defeat, a fast attack with your lightsaber does the trick.

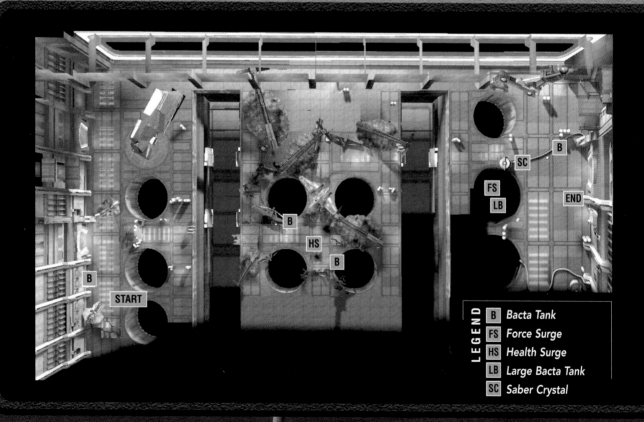

LEGEND
B	Bacta Tank
FS	Force Surge
HS	Health Surge
LB	Large Bacta Tank
SC	Saber Crystal

Because they are not a big threat, experiment with some of the combos by pressing the various attack buttons in different combinations. Also, try pushing the battle droids with your Force power. If you need some health, destroy the explosive containers along the back wall to reveal a bacta tank.

TIP

If you want to see the different combos Anakin can perform, pause the game; at the Pause screen, select the Combat chart.

Just when you are getting the hang of taking on battle droids, you get to take on a super battle droid. This enemy will not fall over with a fast attack. You must use some of those three-button combos. Try ending a combo with a critical attack and hold the thrusting lightsaber in the super battle droid until it is destroyed.

Now follow Obi-Wan to the right. At the platform's edge is another super battle droid. A quick combo knocks it off the edge before you even have to destroy it.

New Objective

• Defeat enemies while R2-D2 extends catwalk

Since you are unable to advance any farther, you must stay put until R2-D2 can extend the catwalk. Be ready to take on groups of battle droids coming at you from the screen's bottom as well as from the left.

If necessary, pick up two bacta tanks that are located in the screen's upper part and lower right corner. Or you can use the Force heal power to convert your Force into health.

After R2-D2 has provided a way to continue, cross over the catwalk to another platform. At the catwalk's end, you must engage a super battle droid. Continue on to attack another super battle droid and a group of battle droids. If you need them, a bacta tank and a large bacta tank are in the area.

TIP

Watch out for the electrical arcs on this area's right side. The arcs can reach out and zap you if you get too close, causing damage. However, you can also use these arcs to your advantage by throwing or pushing enemies into them.

New Objective

• Use the force to clear wreckage

After you clear the area, you must help Obi-Wan clear a wrecked starfighter from your path. Move to the indicated position, then hold down the Force Push button to use the Force to lift the craft out of your way.

SECRET FOUND

Before continuing forward, head back toward the screen's bottom to pick up a secret—a health surge—which increases your maximum amount of health.

Now head up the screen to engage a super battle droid and some more battle droids. Continue to the right and cross another catwalk to the next area.

New Objective

• Shutdown lock-out protocol

Your way out of the hangar is blocked by a shield. As R2-D2 tries to shut it down, you discover that your droid has been locked out. Anakin then jumps down into a landing grid to shut down the lockout. At the bottom, first take out two groups of battle droids that come at you from the left and right. When it is clear, pick up the large bacta tank and the secret Force surge, which increases your maximum Force power. Walk over to the console and interact with it to shut down the lockout. However, before you can leave, you must take out two super battle droids. Stun one while you fight the other. Then destroy the first. To get back to the hangar's upper level, move the indicated point and Force jump to rejoin your friends.

Now fight your way through some battle droids to another Force jump position from which you can jump up onto an elevated platform and take out three battle droid snipers. Don't relax too much since a couple of super battle droids emerge from the doorway. Take out both of them quickly, then Force jump back down to the hangar floor.

New Objective

• Defeat enemies while R2-D2 disables force fields

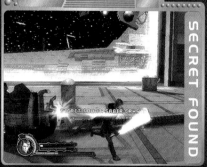

Now you just have to take on the enemies that come at you while R2-D2 opens a way out of the hangar. Before doing anything else, head over to the large container in the upper left and destroy it to reveal a secret—a saber crystal. This automatically fills your Skill meter, preventing enemies from blocking your attacks for a short amount of time and giving you maximum experience points for each enemy you defeat.

Keep attacking the battle droids and a few super battle droids that come at you. There is a bacta tank near the area's top and one at the bottom right. Try throwing the explosive containers at enemies as well to destroy them.

After R2-D2 has disabled the shield, the mission is complete. Anakin and Obi-Wan continue on into the Separatist cruiser while the little astromech droid stays behind in the hangar to provide support as needed.

26

www.lucasarts.com/eps

Mission 2: An Explosive Development

Jedi: Obi-Wan Kenobi

Location: Separatist cruiser

Secrets: 4

As the battle rages over Coruscant, Obi-Wan continues the quest to find the supreme chancellor aboard the Separatist cruiser with help from Anakin Skywalker. But the Jedi are unaware that their every move is being tracked on the ship's command bridge by the leader of the droid forces, General Grievous.

Objective
• Escape the cruiser generator chambers

LEGEND

B	*Bacta Tank*
FS	*Force Surge*
HS	*Health Surge*
LB	*Large Bacta Tank*
SC	*Saber Crystal*

START

END

This time you are Obi-Wan, so keep your eye on the right Jedi. As you and Anakin drop down into the generator chamber, you are immediately faced by two new enemies—grapple droids. These are a bit tougher to destroy than battle droids because their arms are protected by shields that can block your lightsaber. However, they do not shoot at you—they must get in close and hit or grapple with you. After you destroy the two grapple droids, two more drop down for a fight. Take them out as well. There is a bacta tank in this area's upper left if you need to replenish your health.

> ## TIP
>
> Grapple droids tend to block a lot of your strikes. Although it can take a while to destroy them, it does allow you to build up your skill level so you can earn lots of experience points during this mission. Also, try stunning them with the Force, especially if you face more than one. This gives you a chance to get in a good hit before the droid can block.

Now head down a catwalk to the right. Here you must deal with more grapple droids and battle droids. Deal with the battle droids first since they have blasters and attack you from a distance. After clearing them, go after the grapple droids. Stay in this area until the enemy stops coming at you so you can bulk up on skill and experience.

New Objective

- **Disable malfunctioning power node**

As you continue to the right, you come across a power node that is blocking your path with electrical arcs. Face the node, or target it using the right analog stick, and use the saber-throw action to throw your lightsaber and destroy the node.

This will allow Anakin and yourself to continue down the generator chamber's catwalks. Pick up the bacta tank to the power node's right if you need it.

A couple of battle droids come at you as you approach a second malfunctioning power node. Take them out and then use the saber throw to destroy this power node as well. Grab the large bacta tank by the node, then head to a platform with a console. Use the console to extend a catwalk, then help Anakin take on several grapple droids and battle droids. Hit the grapple droids just as they are jumping onto the catwalk—you get in a hit before they can block. This lets you release a quick combo that takes them out before they have a chance to block or strike back.

New Objective

- **Shut down electrical pylons**

After eliminating all of the droids, it is time to continue. However, four electrical pylons block your way. As with the power nodes, target each pylon in turn and throw your lightsaber at it to destroy them; do this until your path to the door at the generator chamber's end is clear. Before running to the catwalk's end, let your Force build up to near its maximum level. You will need it in the next area.

As you enter the next area, you see a couple of battle droids up ahead. Move forward to quickly destroy them, then turn to the left to face a turret suspended from the ceiling. Face the turret; as it begins to fire, hold down the Block button while moving the right analog stick in circles. This causes Obi-Wan to Force deflect the blaster bolts back at the turret. Do this about three times to destroy the turret. Now the grapple droid comes at you. If necessary, pick up the bacta tank on the platform's right side, then go after the droid. Just this one is no trouble for you now. After you defeat the droid, you advance to the next area.

The next area features more catwalks. Head directly to your right to a platform with several crates. Swing at the one on the far right edge to reveal a Force surge secret. However, when you do, a couple of grapple droids jump onto the platform to try to put you in a deadly squeeze. With quick attacks and a little Force stunning, you take them out and get some good skill in the process. If you are hurting after this attack, Force heal yourself. You need health more than Force for the next part of the mission.

Backtrack to this area's start and then head up the ramp to the upper catwalks. You must deal with a few battle droids along the way. When you reach a platform, prepare to take on several grapple droids. Keep up the pressure and eliminate them. If needed, there is a bacta tank on this platform's right side.

New Objective

- Use the Force to bridge the gap

There is a large gap off to the platform's right side—much too far for even a Jedi to jump across. Therefore, you must use your Force powers in another way. Move to the indicated position and press the Force Push button. This causes a large piece of the ship to detach from the wall and serve as a temporary bridge, allowing Anakin and yourself to cross to the catwalk on the opposite side.

New Objective

- Gain access to the service depot

When you jump down onto the catwalks, a couple of grapple droids and some battle droids begin attacking. Eliminate them and any others that show up, then head to the door to the right. It is locked, so use your lightsaber to burn through it. Hold down the Critical Strike button and move the left analog stick left and right to perform the saber plunge. Continue this until you have destroyed the door and can pass to the next area.

When you enter the service depot, grapple droids and battle droids attack you. There are also several explosive containers you can throw at the droids. Just stay away from them or you may get hurt when they blow up. After you neutralize all of the droids, pick up the health surge secret, then destroy the console on the wall to the right. You then find a small locked door. Use the saber plunge once again to continue.

Advance to the right onto a catwalk. When it drops down, you must take out a couple grapple droids. When they are piles of scrap, move to the designated position and Force jump up to the next set of catwalks and continue to the right.

You now face another type of enemy—buzz droids. These little buggers can be a pain once they open up and jump at your head. However, with quick strikes, you can easily destroy them while they are rolling into position. When you reach this point, head back to where the catwalk dropped to find a saber crystal secret. Now continue on to the right. You must destroy a power node and then use the Force to open a large door at the catwalks' end to access the next area.

You will find yourself on a platform with a turret getting ready to fire at you. Use the Force deflect action to destroy the turret with its own firepower. Then go after grapple droids and buzz droids that come to join the party. When it is clear, access the console and pick up the bacta tank. As you head up the ramp to the right, you must deal with another turret. Force deflect until it is eliminated, then access a second console to continue to the next area.

You begin here on a platform with a bacta tank nearby. Pick it up and head to the right. You must fight off a number of grapple droids, battle droids, and buzz droids that come at you from the left and right. Keep up the pressure and don't let up until they are all eliminated.

Head to the right, fighting as you go. You come across a group of three explosive containers off to one side of the main catwalk. Throw your lightsaber at one of them and they will blow up, revealing a health surge secret. Pick it up, then move down the catwalk to the right. When you reach a console, access it to move a walkway toward your location, which allows you to continue on.

New Objective

- Disrupt power to the electrical pylons

There are four electrical pylons that you must destroy. However, before you can concentrate on them, you must deal with a few grapple droids and some buzz droids that come at you. Just concentrate on fighting, then throw your lightsaber at the pylons to clear a path to the right. Continue to the right to complete the mission.

Mission 3: Peril in the Elevators

Briefing

Jedi: Anakin Skywalker

Location: Separatist Cruiser

Secrets: 3

Assisted by Obi-Wan, Anakin continues to Palpatine's location on the cruiser's upper levels, determined to retrieve the chancellor from Grievous' clutches. Continued pursuit from the ship's patrolling droids threatens the Jedi, while R2-D2 attempts to aid the Jedi in their ascent.

Objective
- Take elevator to the cruiser throne room
- Defeat destroyer droids

Walkthrough

You are in control of Anakin. Get ready for some action right at the beginning. You face a new enemy—destroyer droids. These have a lot of firepower, and they are protected by shields. Use your Force stun ability to temporarily shut down their shields so you can move in and turn them into scrap.

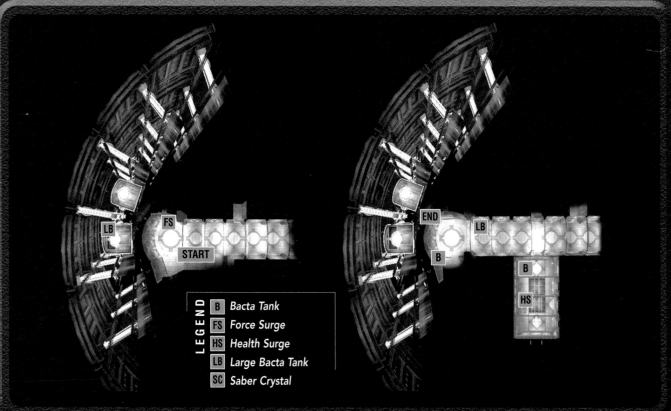

LB

FS

START

END

LB

B

B

HS

LEGEND

B	Bacta Tank
FS	Force Surge
HS	Health Surge
LB	Large Bacta Tank
SC	Saber Crystal

As you head toward the elevator, strike at the round hatch on the wall at the back of the area. This reveals a Force surge secret.

New Objective

• Enter elevator

To get into the elevator, you must cut through the door. To do a saber cut, hold down the Critical Strike button and then move the left analog stick in the direction you want to cut. Work the saber around in a clockwise motion to create an opening into the elevator.

Anakin and Obi-Wan will automatically enter the elevator. As buzz droids start to drop in on you, Anakin jumps up onto the elevator's top. When you regain control of Anakin, begin attacking the buzz droids as they appear at the edges of the elevator. This is not very difficult. Just keep moving around and slashing at them before they can attack you.

After a period, air battle droids, located on the top of another elevator, begin to attack you. Anakin jumps across to engage them. You must take on three at once in the beginning of this battle. However, there is a large bacta tank in the upper right corner if you need some health.

TIP

Air battle droids are outfitted with an arm shield with which they can block your lightsaber. While you can stun them, a better tactic is to grapple them and then throw them off the elevator. However, if you want to get more skill and eventually more experience, go at them with the lightsaber, stunning as needed. Also try to attack these droids as they are landing and before they can activate their arm shields.

New Objective

• Reunite with Obi-Wan

If you stand in the elevator's upper left corner for a few seconds, a saber crystal secret appears. Pick it up; then you can really go after the grapple droids that climb up from the elevator car below. Again, grapple and throw these droids off the elevator if you want to quickly dispose of them.

As you complete the destruction of the grapple droids, some buzz droids climb up to attack you. Keep fighting them off until R2-D2 can get you to the same level as Obi-Wan.

When you and Obi-Wan are reunited, you must fight off some more destroyer droids. As before, stun and then attack. There is also a large bacta tank along the left wall if you need it.

New Objective

• Locate controls and disable force field

Ray shields will drop down, sealing you into this corridor as more destroyer droids come to attack. Locate a locked door along the right side and use your lightsaber to cut your way inside.

PRIMA OFFICIAL GAME GUIDE

As you enter this room, pick up the bacta tank in the corner on the left. Buzz droids attack you here. Fight them off until you defeat them all.

SECRET FOUND

Along the room's left side is an explosive container. Either throw your saber at it or throw the container to reveal a health surge secret. Now head over to the console on the room's other side and access it to disable the force field.

A turret lowers right in front of the door through which you must exit. Force deflect the shots back at the turret to destroy it, then exit the room to join up with Obi-Wan again.

On the elevator, you must fight off some buzz droids and lots of air battle droids that fly in to attack you. Attack them near the edges, pushing them off; or, attack them when they land, hitting them before they can activate their arm shields.

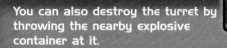

TIP

You can also destroy the turret by throwing the nearby explosive container at it.

As you exit, you must help Obi-Wan fight off some grapple droids. If you need health, there is a large bacta tank along the right wall and another bacta tank near the elevators.

After you neutralize all of the droids, head toward the elevators at the back of this area and the two Jedi jump down into the shaft and onto an elevator.

After you defeat all th
droids, Obi-Wan and
Anakin drop back
down into the elevato
and continue to the
next mission.

Mission 4: Settling the Score

Briefing

Jedi: Anakin Skywalker

Location: Separatist cruiser

Secrets: 2

With some help from R2-D2, Anakin leads Obi-Wan to their final destination, and the Jedi are poised to liberate the chancellor. The only thing blocking their path is a stately former Jedi named Count Dooku, who is now the Sith Lord known as Darth Tyranus.

Objective

- Defeat Count Dooku (Darth Tyranus)
- Rescue Chancellor Palpatine

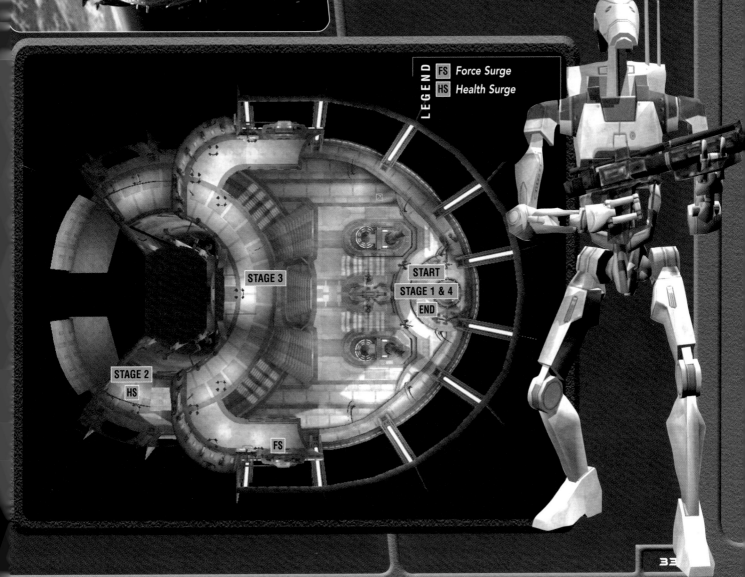

LEGEND

FS *Force Surge*
HS *Health Surge*

STAGE 3

START

STAGE 1 & 4

END

STAGE 2

HS

FS

Walkthrough

This is your first duel. You fight against Count Dooku the entire time, and the duel takes place in four stages. To begin with, you have Obi-Wan to assist you.

In order to win, you must develop the shunt tactic. This is essentially a parry where you block and knock aside your enemy's lightsaber and follow up with an attack of your own. To do this, block and move toward your opponent as he attacks. Then follow up with either a quick or strong slash of your own while he is open.

Also try using some of your Force powers. A saber throw is a good way to attack Count Dooku at a distance and still cause some damage. You can also use Force grasp to lift up your opponent and throw him to cause damage. The key to this first stage of the duel is to avoid taking much damage yourself. Keep your distance if you get hurt, and Force heal while assisting Obi-Wan with ranged attacks.

When Count Dooku's health is at about three-quarters of its maximum, the second stage of the duel begins. You move onto an upper walkway area. However, Count Dooku has immobilized Obi-Wan under a structure in the room. You are on your own for the rest of the duel, and Count Dooku shows you some of his more advanced moves now.

> **TIP**
> If you need to heal up, Force push or throw Count Dooku to buy you a few seconds to Force heal yourself. This is the one power for which you want to keep some Force on hand.

When both you and Count Dooku make a strong slash at each other, your lightsabers will lock. Quickly press both Quick and Strong Slash buttons simultaneously to push back on your opponent and open him up to an attack.

This level also has large cylindrical objects hanging from the wall. Target them with the Force and then throw them at your opponent to break up his attacks and cause more damage.

Head around to this area's far left end and attack the console to reveal a secret—a Force surge. Use up as much of your Force with saber throws and other attacks so that when you pick up this secret, it does you some good.

SECRET FOUND

After you reduce Count Dooku's health to about half, he leads you to the duel's third stage, on another walkway area. However, since he is not doing so well, the Count calls up some reinforcements. Pairs of super battle droids emerge from the doors at the ends of the walkways. Since these droids can shoot at you from a distance, go after them before continuing the duel.

Use the super battle droids against Count Dooku. Put him between you and the droids, and then either Force deflect their shots at Dooku or Force throw the droids at him. This takes care of the droids and puts the hurt on your opponent.

Knock a super battle droid over the railing in the center of the room with your saber or a Force power, then head to the walkway's left side to find a secret health surge. There is no other health in this mission, so grab it.

SECRET FOUND

Look for openings wherever they appear. Be ready to block or shunt Count Dooku's attacks. However, as he reaches an end of a slash or combo, be ready with one of your own and let him have it.

The final stage back in front of the chancellor begins when Count Dooku has only about a quarter of his health remaining. Luckily the super battle droids do not make any more appearances. However, Count Dooku is still a deadly threat on his own, so don't let your guard down.

With a little more room to work with, use saber throws to keep your opponent off balance in between slashing attacks. He does not have much health left and every hit counts.

PRESS Ⓑ TO PERFORM A LUNGE ATTACK

As he gets weaker, Count Dooku is more susceptible to critical strikes such as the lunge attack. Use this as a third button of a combo and hold it if you connect for maximum damage.

After you have taken away all of Count Dooku's health, Anakin finishes the duel—and finishes a Sith Lord. He then frees Chancellor Palpatine to complete the mission.

Mission 5: It's Not Over Yet

Briefing

Jedi: Anakin Skywalker

Location: Separatist Cruiser

Secrets: 3

There is a sinister mood as Palpatine witnesses Anakin's flirtation with the dark side while getting revenge on Count Dooku. The young Jedi must now lead the chancellor and Obi-Wan toward the cruiser's hangar. But the furious combat outside begins to take its toll on the Separatist flagship, and R2-D2 again needs to aid in the rescue.

Objective
- **Reunite with Obi-Wan and Palpatine**

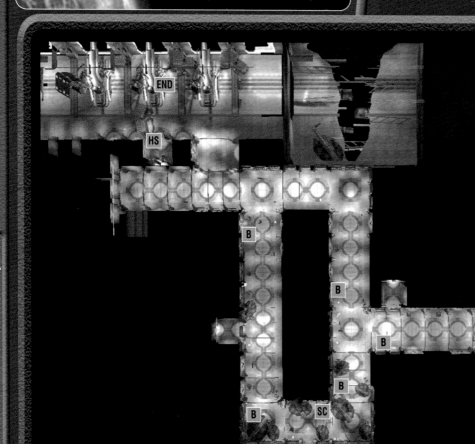

LEGEND

B	Bacta Tank
FS	Force Surge
HS	Health Surge
LB	Large Bacta Tank
SC	Saber Crystal

Walkthrough

As Anakin leads Obi-Wan and the chancellor, he finds himself alone as a ray shield separates the party. You are on your own. While trapped in this corridor, take out some battle droids that come at you from the front and a few super battle droids that approach from the back. Go after the battle droids, because they pass through the ray shields first. If the super battle droids start shooting, Force deflect their shots or stun them as you advance to destroy them.

After you clear the corridor, a ray shield opens, allowing you to continue. Get ready for more battle droids and a destroyer droid. Stun the destroyer to drop its shields and then slash away.

New Objective

- Locate controls and disable force field

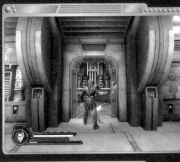

In order to get through the next force field, you must find a control room. Along the wall near the force field is a door. As you approach, it opens automatically. Slash at the cables at the rear of the room to drop the force field.

As you exit the control room, be ready for a turret and lots of droids. In fact, if your Force meter is low, wait in the room until it builds back up. Then head out and Force deflect blaster bolts back at the turret and the super battle droids. By the time the turret is destroyed, most of the droids are as well. Before you continue, pick up the bacta tank along the corridor's left side.

TIP

There are several explosive containers near the turret. Try using the Force to throw them at the turret and the droids in the area.

Move into the intersection and locate a panel to the right of the destroyed turret. Cut into the panel to reveal circuitry. Slash at it to lower the force field to your right, allowing you to advance. As you head to the right, pick up a bacta tank along the wall.

New Objective

- Escort R2-D2
- Defeat enemies while R2-D2 disables force fields

As you head down the corridor, you confront several super battle droids. However, the cruiser takes a hit and these droids are sucked out into the vacuum of space. A force field drops down and prevents you from flying out as well. It also blocks your path. Turn around and head to the left. Be ready to stun a destroyer droid as soon as you see it and then slash away to finish it off. As the corridor turns to the right, watch out for electrical arcs. Also destroy the crate near the corner to reveal a bacta tank.

As you round the corner, slash at a crate on the right side to reveal a saber crystal secret. Then get ready to Force deflect the fire from a turret at the corridor's end. Move forward and destroy any remaining droids.

SECRET FOUND

There is a second secret in this area. Locate a door on the corridor's left side before you come to the intersection. Cut through the door with your lightsaber to reveal a health surge. Pick it up and then continue to the intersection. Cut the panel on the right side and slash at the cables to lower this force field so you can advance to the right.

As you approach another force field, take on some super battle droids. Deflect their shots as you close and then let them have it.

The controls to the force field are located in a small room near the field. This time, electrical arcs block your path. Target the cables and then throw your lightsaber to cut them and lower the force field.

At the corridor's end is yet another turret. You can either deflect its shots or use the Force to throw an explosive container at the turret to destroy it. There is also a bacta tank along the left wall. You now have to wait while R2-D2 lowers the force field.

There are several droids on the other side. A few battle droids move through the field; attack them and cover R2-D2.

TIP

Although you can't move through the force field, your Force powers can. Try picking up and throwing droids. You can even destroy super battle droids using only the Force. Pick them up and throw them at a force field to turn them into scrap metal.

OBJECTIVE ACHIEVED: DEFEAT ENEMIES WHILE R2 DISABLES FORCE FIELDS

When the force field is down, go after the destroyer droids. Stun them to lower their shields or use Force deflect. Since they can fire through their shields, their blaster bolts reflect right back through the shields as well, destroying these dangerous droids. As you approach Obi-Wan and the chancellor, more destroyer droids appear. Take them all out to continue to the next area.

New Objective

• Enter gun battery

As you enter the gun battery, you must take out several battle droids. However, before you approach the cannon, turn to the left to locate a locked door. Cut through it with your lightsaber and enter to pick up a health surge secret.

You fire at three different sections of the enemy ship. Keep shooting at each section until the targeting reticule changes and the ship is eventually destroyed.

With your last objective accomplished, the mission is complete. However, you are not getting off the Separatist cruiser just yet.

New Objective

• Use cannon to defeat banking clan ship

Now approach and mount the cannon to begin supporting your allies by firing at the Separatist ship.

Mission 6: The General's Right Hand

Briefing

Jedi: Anakin Skywalker

Location: Separatist Cruiser

Secrets: 2

Their escape foiled, the Jedi and Palpatine are brought before the dreaded General Grievous, who is flanked by his formidable bodyguards. Down but not out, Anakin and Obi-Wan still have a few tricks remaining in their rescue mission. Hopefully the Separatist cruiser stays in orbit long enough for them to be used.

Objective
- Defeat Grievous' bodyguards

Walkthrough

This mission is similar to a duel. However, instead of fighting a single opponent, you take on several at once. For the first stage, you take on Grievous' bodyguards and some battle droids.

LEGEND

B	Bacta Tank
FS	Force Surge
HS	Health Surge
LB	Large Bacta Tank

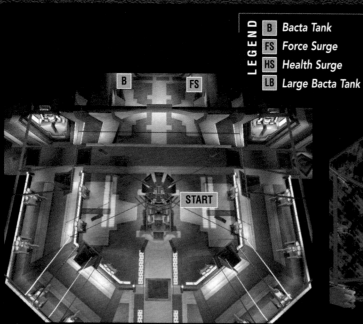

The bodyguards are armed with power staffs, which are similar to lightsabers. These staffs can block your lightsaber and cause damage when they hit. Keep your lightsaber up in a block stance and be ready to shunt the blows and move in for an attack of your own.

SECRET FOUND

If you move to the area's back, near the large door to the ship's bridge, slash at the console on the right wall to reveal a Force surge secret. Slash at the console on the left wall to get a bacta tank.

Use your Force powers during this fight. Throwing or pushing Grievous' bodyguards disrupts their lightning-fast attacks and gives you a chance to get in some slashes of your own.

After you clear off the droids on the bridge, the cruiser turns on its side, leaving Anakin and Obi-Wan fighting on glass. To begin with, you must deal with several grapple droids and some battle droids. The grapple droids give you a chance to build up your skill and experience, so stay on the offensive and keep slashing away until you destroy them.

Grievous' bodyguards join the fight after a bit. Since you have such a small area in which to fight, be careful that two droids at a time don't surround you. Stay near the edges so you can keep the enemies to your front.

TIP

Force push or throw droids into other droids. Because of the close confines, it is pretty easy to hit another droid and cause damage to two droids for the cost of a single use of the Force.

Battle droids appear at the screen's bottom, so as you move about the area, be ready to slash at them when they come into range. A quick Force push also destroys them from a distance and prevents them from firing at you. However, you must really concentrate on the bodyguards since they offer the most danger to you.

After clearing out the glass area, the cruiser tilts again so that the bridge is inverted. You are now fighting on the ceiling against Grievous' bodyguards, grapple droids, and battle droids.

SECRET FOUND

By this time, you need some health. Make your way to the area's right side and slash at a console to reveal a secret health surge. If you need more health later, there is a large bacta tank in the bridge's back left.

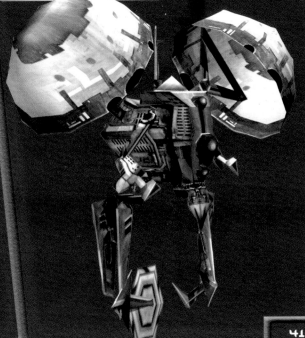

You have a lot more room to maneuver in this area. However, most of the fighting takes place near the bridge's center. Move in for the fight, but be careful. It is easy to be surrounded.

Try to lure or Force push individual enemies toward the area's sides so that you can duel them one on one. Then as it begins to thin out, move into the center again for some more action. If you can back the bodyguards up against a structure, you limit their ability to move out of the way of your lightsaber slashes.

With a little more room, throwing your lightsaber is a good tactic to cause damage without having to get into a major fight in the middle of the bridge.

TIP

While Obi-Wan can take care of himself, it is a good idea to get behind the droid he is fighting. This often allows you to get in some quick slashes that won't be blocked and then allows both Obi-Wan and yourself to move on to other droids.

After you eliminate all the droids on the bridge, only General Grievous remains. However, he decides to escape rather than take on two Jedi. Anakin now gets Obi-Wan, Chancellor Palpatine, and himself off of the Separatist cruiser and to safety.

Mission 1: Investigating Utapau

Briefing

Jedi: Obi-Wan Kenobi

Location: Utapau

Secrets: 3

Objective
- Destroy Separatist opposition
- Infiltrate control sphere

Walkthrough

Obi-Wan and Anakin get the chancellor safely back to Coruscant, ending the Separatist ploy. With Dooku defeated, the Jedi Council doubles its efforts to bring General Grievous to justice. Tracking Grievous to the Utapau system, the Council sends Obi-Wan after the Separatist leader, this time without the aid of Anakin. Already frustrated by the Council, Anakin is further dismayed to learn that Mace Windu suspects Chancellor Palpatine is behind the perpetuation of the Clone Wars. The conflicted young Jedi is now stuck on Coruscant, faced with the growing divide between his friend and mentor, the chancellor, and the Jedi Order—without the guidance of Obi-Wan, who begins his daring mission on Utapau.

This mission has a lot of variety. You take on several different types of enemies and use many of the skills and abilities at your disposal. Start off by heading along the catwalks, taking out battle droids as you go. There are also a few super battle droids.

LEGEND

B	*Bacta Tank*
FS	*Force Surge*
HS	*Health Surge*
LB	*Large Bacta Tank*

Walk down the first catwalk to the left toward a door blocked by a force field. Target the power node up and to the left and throw your lightsaber at it. This shuts down the force field and allows you to enter a room; pick up a Force surge secret.

Continue down the catwalk to the platform. There is a turret over the door. Take it out by Force deflecting its shots as quickly as possible because you are going to have company really soon. Grapple droids show up and attack. To deal with them, stun them first, then attack. After you eliminate all the droids in this area, head through the doorway to the next area.

> **TIP**
>
> To maximize your skill and experience, don't stun the grapple droids because you want to get as many hits on them as possible. Even blocked hits yield skill, so slash away if you want to really upgrade your character at the mission's end.

Follow the catwalk, eliminating battle droids, super battle droids, and grapple droids along the way. Try a Force deflect since most of the enemy fire comes from one direction. This takes care of most of the droids for you.

There is a battle droid sniper located on the large pipe at the area's far right edge. To get rid of it, target the droid and then Force throw it off the pipe. That saves you some unwanted loss of health. Now move to the indicated position and Force jump up to the next level.

You land on a section of catwalk that contains several buzz droids. Eliminate them all, then access the console to bring another section of the catwalk down into place so you can continue. This section, however, contains a super battle droid and a couple battle droids. Quickly defeat them and advance.

New Objective

- **Shut down heat vents**

Now a heat vent blocks your path. Its power node is located along the wall. Target it and throw your lightsaber to shut down the vents, allowing you to pass. You also find a large bacta tank here, which you could probably use by now.

New Objective

- **Operate lift controls**

At the catwalk's end is a console. Use the controls to move another platform into position. Before you can Force jump over to it, you must defeat some buzz droids and grapple droids.

On the platform, you must take on several air battle droids. Stay there until you defeat them all. Then you must get past two heat vents. Stand next to the flame jet, then run past as it stops momentarily.

At the far end, destroy a crate to reveal a bacta tank and let your Force recharge. When it reaches its maximum, Force jump to the next level. You must Force run again to get past the cannon and to safety on the other side.

In between the second and third vents is a power node. Throw your lightsaber at it to shut down the vents so you can reach the platform on the other side. There you must throw an explosive container at a turret before a grapple droid arrives to attack. Eliminate it and other droids that arrive. If you need some health, pick up the large bacta tank hiding behind the crates. Then cut your way through the locked door to enter the next area.

New Objective

• Utilize Separatist cannon

SECRET FOUND

In this room you face a grapple droid and a couple battle droids. Others also arrive to take you on. When it is clear, slash at the horizontal pipes along the left wall to access an alcove and a health surge secret. This really comes in handy about now. Finally, cut your way through a locked door to exit the room.

The next cannon is not manned. Therefore, you can take your time, fighting off battle droids and super battle droids as you approach the cannon. Access the console across from the large force field to move a catwalk over to the cannon. Then climb on the cannon and get ready for some shooting. If you need health, grab the large bacta tank near the cannon before using the cannon.

MOVE L TWICE IN A DIRECTION TO USE FORCE SPEED

You must now deal with a large cannon that is shooting at you. Don't try to Force deflect it. Instead, Force run along the catwalks as much as possible. If you have to stop, do so behind a crate or container. These block only one shot, so move out after the shot until you get around a corner where the cannon can't hit you.

New Objective

• Destroy force field nodes

As you man the cannon, use the left analog stick to aim. The Quick Slash button fires quick blasts while the Strong Slash button fires charged shots. Aim at the nodes on either side of the force field. Watch your heat level in the screen's lower right corner. When the cannon gets too hot, it can't fire until it cools down. Use charged shots at the nodes and quick blasts at the droids that come at you. They can cause you damage, so quickly engage them. After you destroy the nodes, you automatically dismount from the cannon. Take out the droids and head for the doorway, picking up the large bacta tank as you run past.

Past the corner, you take on more droids. However, don't keep going. Behind the doorway with the force field is a large bacta tank. To shut down the force field, target the power node above the door, then jump and throw your lightsaber at it. You must back away from the door in order for this to work. When you have the bacta tank, run past another cannon. Let your Force build up before you try this so you can Force run most of the way to cover at the other side.

New Objective

- Defeat crab droid

You must now destroy a crab droid. This is not easy. When you are at a distance, it fires at you. Jump out of the shot's way. Up close, it tries to hit you with its claws. To defeat it, get near its head and grapple it. This puts you onto its back where you can get in a few slashes. The crab droid's health meter is in the screen's upper right corner, allowing you to see how much more it can take.

If you start getting low on health, use Force heal or head to the area's left side near where you entered. Slash at the crates to reveal a health surge secret.

You must climb onto the crab droid several times. Don't try to jump onto its back— grappling from the front is the only way to get there. After it bucks you off, get ready to jump out of the way of a shot and then move in for another grapple. Eventually, through perseverance, you destroy the crab droid, allowing Obi-Wan to continue his assignment on Utapau.

Mission B: The Cavalry Arrives

Briefing

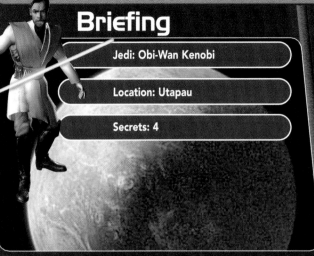

Jedi: Obi-Wan Kenobi

Location: Utapau

Secrets: 4

After successfully navigating the Separatist stronghold, Obi-Wan Kenobi locates Grievous and must apprehend the general to complete his mission and end the Clone Wars. However, in order to flush out Grievous, Obi-Wan must face not only his bodyguards, but also endless waves of droid forces without the help of his clone army.

Objective

- Defeat Grievous' bodyguards
- Capture General Grievous

Walkthrough

This mission is somewhat similar to the last mission on the Separatist cruiser. You must fight off Grievous' bodyguards as well as other droids. However, you do not have another Jedi to help you. Your first task is to defeat Grievous' bodyguards in a large open area. As soon as you do, the mission moves to the next stage, so concentrate on the two bodyguards.

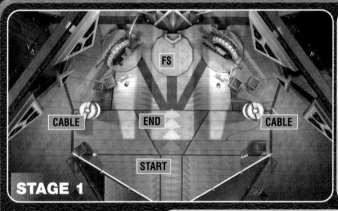

STAGE 1

STAGE 2

LEGEND

B	Bacta Tank
FS	Force Surge
HS	Health Surge
LB	Large Bacta Tank
SC	Saber Crystal

STAGE 3

TIP

Grievous' bodyguards can be deadly up close. Try to soften them up by throwing your lightsaber at them from a distance and using Force push and throw.

You find the first secret at the mission's start. Off to the left and right sides are power cables. Target them and throw your lightsaber to destroy them. After you hit both, a Force surge secret appears in the back area.

New Objective

• Assist clone invasion

The mission's second stage takes part in a control room. However, the clones have begun their invasion, and you have their assistance. You face lots of battle droids and grapple droids in this area.

There is a bacta tank on the left side and a second one on the right side. Keep fighting off the droids until the clone gunships are ready to bring in reinforcements. The danger here is that you must focus on the grapple droids while also being aware of battle droids firing at you.

Therefore, it is a good idea to stun the grapple droids and finish them off quickly rather than slash away for skill and experience.

This area also contains a secret. If you destroy all of the control consoles at the area's far end, you earn a saber crystal. Since this gives you instant maximum skill for experience, go for this near the beginning of this area.

New Objective

• Disable cannons firing on clone gunships

You receive word from the clone gunships that they are being attacked by Separatist cannons. Luckily, you can disable them from within the control room. Toward the rear of the area are two Force jump locations. Head to the one on the left and jump up to the balcony.

After fighting off battle droids and grapple droids, access the console to lower the shield over the generator. Then use your lightsaber to destroy the generator to disable half of the cannons.

While you are here, look up to find power cables along the wall at the back. Target them, then jump and throw your lightsaber to destroy them. This gives you a health surge secret on the balcony over by the console. Pick it up and then jump back down to the control room's main floor.

Now head to the next Force jump location and jump up to the balcony on the right. Do the same thing you did on the other balcony to disable the rest of the cannons. Unfortunately, there is no secret on this side.

Now jump down to the main floor again to continue fighting off the droids until you get new orders. If you need health, there is a large bacta tank near the edge of the area.

New Objective

- Locate shield controls for the control sphere

The clone troops can't land in the control sphere until you lower the shields. Therefore, you have a new area in which to operate. More of Grievous' bodyguards are here as well as other droids. Your objectives are the power cables at the rear of the area, both on the right and the left. Cutting these with your lightsaber allows you to access the shield controls.

> **TIP**
>
> There are several explosive containers in this area along the sides. Throw them at the more powerful droids. You can even throw the battle droids at other droids.

SECRET FOUND

Destroy the console at the area's front right to earn a Force surge secret. This can come in handy if you have been doing a lot of saber throws, Force throws, or stuns against the droids.

New Objective

- Destroy shield controls with the Force

When the doors to the shield controls are opened, two turrets descend from the ceiling and begin shooting at you. Since you have droids coming at you from all directions, it can be difficult to Force deflect the turret shots. So, either throw an explosive container at the turrets or throw your lightsaber to destroy them. This works especially well if you have upgraded your saber-throw ability.

Keep fighting the droids to clear out this area as much as possible. Make sure you eliminate all of the Grievous' bodyguards and the grapple droids. Battle droids continue to enter, so get as many as possible before going after the controls. Then head to the rear of the area and stand at the designated location; use the Force to destroy the controls.

New Objective

- Defeat crab droid

With the shields down, the clone troopers arrive. However, the Separatists have one more problem for you to handle—a crab droid. What makes this one tougher is that you also have battle droids shooting at you and getting in the way.

As before, jump out of the way of the crab droid's fire, then rush in and grapple to get on top. Slash away while you can and then get back up when you are bucked off. A couple bacta tanks are at the area's sides if you need to restore your health. Also Force heal as needed. After you defeat the crab, the mission is complete.

Mission 9: Showdown with Grievous

Briefing

Jedi: Obi-Wan Kenobi

Location: Utapau

Secrets: 2

In the chaos of the Separatists' defeat on Utapau, General Grievous attempts to escape, racing toward his hidden starship. With help from Commander Cody, Obi-Wan catches sight of the fleeing droid and mounts a pursuit on the back of a native boga lizard, chasing Grievous toward their final showdown.

Objective
- Defeat General Grievous

Walkthrough

This is another duel mission. It is just you and General Grievous. Though you bested Count Dooku earlier, Grievous is much more deadly. This droid is armed with two lightsabers and can bring out an additional two when desired.

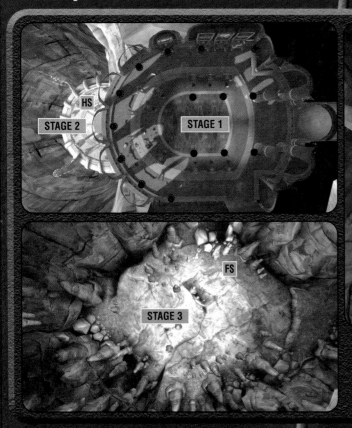

STAGE 2

HS

STAGE 1

STAGE 3

FS

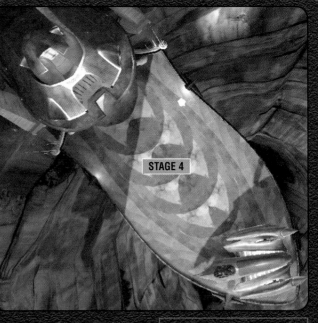

STAGE 4

LEGEND
FS Force Surge
HS Health Surge

Be ready to Force heal as necessary. Just move a distance away from your opponent and heal up. The Force push is also a good tactic against Grievous. While the droid is not really stunned, the push opens it up so you can get in a quick combo without being blocked, or at least prevent Grievous from hitting you while coming to attack.

The key to winning this duel is to avoid letting Grievous hit you with combos. The general has some pretty powerful attacks that can cause a lot of damage if they connect with you.

Your safest tactic is to stay at a distance and cause as much ranged damage as possible. The control room has several chairs that you can throw at Grievous. In addition, try throwing your lightsaber to get in a few quick hits. This can also disrupt your opponent as the droid sets up an attack.

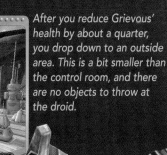

After you reduce Grievous' health by about a quarter, you drop down to an outside area. This is a bit smaller than the control room, and there are no objects to throw at the droid.

The good news about this area is that there is a secret. Head to the far right and start slashing at the structures on this rooftop to reveal a health surge; you can probably really use it about now.

Get Grievous' health down to half and the droid runs away. Obi-Wan follows to resume the duel in a cavern. The stalagmites on the floor make this area small and confining.

Slash away at stalagmites in the area's right rear to earn a Force surge secret. Force heal before you pick it up to maximize its usefulness.

Watch out for Grievous' pistol. At times, the droid pulls it out for a quick shot at you. Block it with your lightsaber.

Keep up the pressure on the droid. Use Force push frequently to keep your opponent off balance and to allow you to get in a few hits.

When you have General Grievous down to only a quarter health, the duel moves to a landing platform. This is where the droid is most dangerous. Saber throws work well to get in a few quick hits. You don't need all that much more to finish him off.

When Grievous is on the attack, block and shunt the blows. If possible, Force push the droid away from you to stop the attack, or at least move it away from you.

One powerful attack the General uses requires him to kneel down before a fast running strike. When you see this, prepare to jump to the side since the attack advances in a straight line. Then get ready to hit your opponent with an attack of your own at the end.

When Grievous goes down, move in for some quick hits to finish him off. However, be careful since the general may be preparing to strike back.

Keep up the pressure, fighting very defensively during this final stage. If you do so, you defeat this Separatist general and bring the Clone Wars to an end.

TIP

By completing this mission, you unlock General Grievous for multiplayer duels. Try this character out, especially the droid's special attacks, to see why it was such a tough fight.

Mission 10: The Dark Side of the Force

Briefing

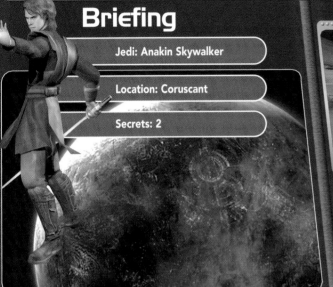

Jedi: Anakin Skywalker

Location: Coruscant

Secrets: 2

Meanwhile, on Coruscant, Mace Windu gathers incriminating information against Palpatine and confronts the chancellor in his quarters. It's there that Palpatine reveals his true identity as the Sith Lord who's controlling the Galactic Senate. Just as Mace is about to strike Palpatine down, a bewildered Anakin enters the room and sees his friend on the wrong end of what appears to be a Jedi assassination attempt.

Objective
• Defeat Mace Windu

Walkthrough

This mission, like the previous one, is also a duel. However, this time it is Jedi versus Jedi. Mace Windu is a Jedi Master, so be ready for a good fight. Mace has a lot of moves and will press the attack up close or at range.

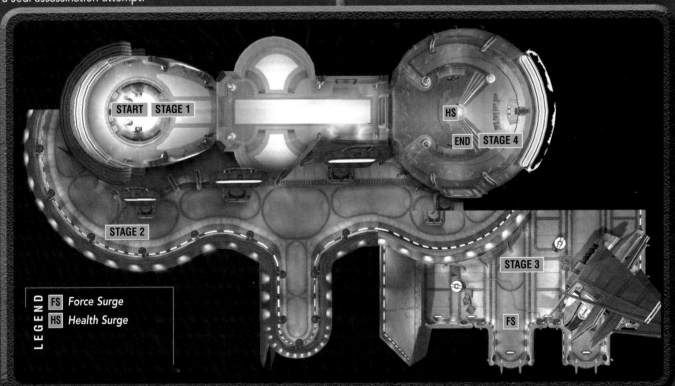

START STAGE 1

HS

END STAGE 4

STAGE 2

STAGE 3

FS

LEGEND
FS *Force Surge*
HS *Health Surge*

The first area of this mission, the chancellor's office, has several pieces of furniture to throw at your opponent. Do this early in the duel to put the hurt on Mace and give you an early advantage. If you don't use the furniture, it is destroyed when lightsabers slash through the office.

TIP

Mace Windu tries to use his Force powers to stun you. When this happens, quickly press your Quick Slash and Strong Slash buttons to break the mental attack.

While your opponent is too powerful in the Force to stun, you can use the Force to push and throw him. This gives you a chance to set up an attack, catch your breath, or just cause some additional damage to Mace.

When you get into a saber lock, quickly press your two Slash buttons simultaneously. This causes Anakin to push back Mace Windu and then perform a quick attack against the Jedi Master. If you can push Mace up against a wall, attack him as he slides down it to the ground. Another tactic is to pick up Mace and pull him toward you, slashing at him while he is in the air and defenseless.

After taking away a quarter of Windu's health, he jumps out of the office window to a balcony area below. Anakin follows to continue the duel. This area is filled with objects that you can throw at Mace, so use them to your advantage.

There are also a couple places where electrical arcs reach out from the edges. You can either try to back your opponent into one of these and then Force push him, or you can pick up Mace and throw him into the arcs for additional damage.

Since this area is much larger—it continues along a narrow walkway to the right—you can move away from Mace to Force heal or to set up an opportunity to throw something at him.

SECRET FOUND

Get Mace down to half health and you move to a landing platform. Destroy the computer console on the right side and the two on the left to reveal a Force surge secret out in the area's middle.

This area has less objects to throw, so you must get in close and take on Mace with your lightsaber. Remember to keep up your block and launch your own combos as Mace is finishing one of his own.

TIP

Mace tries to Force heal in this third area. Don't let him or you will just have to cause more damage to end the duel. When he does this, either start slashing if you are close or throw your lightsaber if at a distance. You may even want to pull him closer using the Force.

Keep up the pressure on Windu, always staying on the attack when you can and defending when he attacks you. If you have earned new attacks through upgrading, try them out. These come in handy as the duel approaches the end.

Back in a small area again, try to keep Mace up against a wall or move down the steps and box him in near some furniture so he can't pull away from your attacks. If you knock your opponent down, either with a combo or with a Force throw, move in and go for a critical strike—but be ready for him to jump up and attack.

Knowing he does not have much health left, Mace jumps back up into the chancellor's office to finish off Palpatine. However, Anakin also returns to defend his friend.

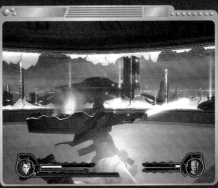

Stay on the offensive and you eventually defeat the great Jedi Master and save the chancellor. However, Anakin has made a decisive move toward the dark side of the Force.

SECRET FOUND

Destroy the five light pylons (three near the stairs and two with the statues) to release a very welcome health surge secret. By this time in the duel, this gives you the strength to finish off Mace Windu.

SECRET FOUND: HEALTH SURGE: MAX HEALTH INCREASE

Mission 11: The Hunt Begins

Briefing

Jedi: Anakin Skywalker

Location: Coruscant

Secrets: 5

Having made his choice in striking at Mace Windu, Anakin places all of his trust with Palpatine, who goes to work on Anakin, playing on his fears and anxieties. The crafty Sith Lord manipulates Anakin into believing that the Jedi Order betrayed the Republic and him, and that Obi-Wan is equally complicit. The chancellor's words are powerful, and they sway the young Jedi. Anakin swears his allegiance to Palpatine—and to the dark side of the Force.

Seduced by his newfound power, the newly christened Darth Vader is sent to the Jedi Temple on a quest to send the traitorous Jedi to their doom.

Objective
- Exterminate Jedi
- Set temple beacon

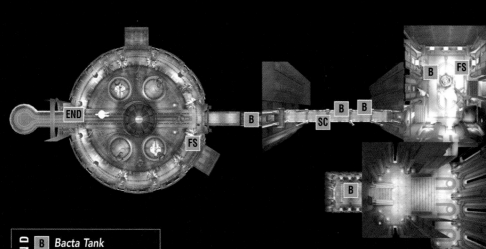
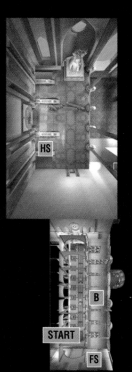

LEGEND

B	Bacta Tank
FS	Force Surge
HS	Health Surge
LB	Large Bacta Tank
SC	Saber Crystal

Walkthrough

You begin the mission in the Jedi library. While there are several Jedi you must defeat here, they are all Padawans and little challenge for a Jedi Knight such as Anakin. If you have upgraded and have new attacks, this is the perfect time to test them out.

TIP

Since he has turned to the dark side, Anakin's Force stun has changed to Force lightning. This attack causes damage to the target, and a sustained blast can even kill a Padawan.

Move to the far right back wall in the library corridor to find a Force surge secret.

New Objective

- Disengage library force fields

After defeating some of the enemies, a Jedi rushes into a control room on the upper balcony and engages a force field, sealing you in the library. Locate the indicated position and then Force jump up onto the balcony. Eliminate the Padawans up there, then cut your way into the panel to the right of the sealed doorway. Slash at the power cables to lower the shields. There is a Jedi inside who comes out to attack you. Deal with him, then enter the room and access the console to shut down the force fields. Before jumping back down to the library's ground level, pick up the bacta tank. You must now fight off more Padawans as you head to the door at the area's left side. Clone troopers help you in your effort; you have little trouble.

As you exit into the courtyard, you face several more Jedi. Watch out for the male humans since these Jedi will throw their lightsabers at you.

New Objective

- Use the Force to access the study hall

Move to the area's left side, near the front, to reveal a health surge secret. Consider not moving to this area until you really need it.

After defeating the Jedi, move toward the statue at the courtyard's far end. While standing on the designated spot, use your Force powers to topple the statue, then use it to break open the door to the study hall.

Enter the study hall and defeat the Jedi located there. They put up a good fight, but it is nothing compared to the power of the dark side. There is also a bacta tank in here.

New Objective

- Shut down study hall force fields

The doorway through which you want to exit is blocked by a force field, so head to the locked door at the area's far end and plunge your lightsaber in to cut it open. In the next area is a Jedi with a double-bladed lightsaber. This one is tough—most of your Force powers will not faze him. However, if you have some upgraded attacks, this is a good time to use them. This opponent is very fast, so don't try to mix it up with only standard slashes and blocks.

TIP

Get this Jedi up against a wall and then Force grasp him. This gives you a bit of an opening in which to land a quick slash and a possible combo before he can block you.

Continue through the door to the control room. Make sure you have a full Force meter, since you need to Force deflect two turrets that hang from the ceiling. After you destroy them, access the console to shut down the force fields and pick up a bacta tank.

As you exit the control room and head back to the study hall, you confront a few more Jedi. However, you now have some clone troopers to help you deal with them.

When you return to the study hall, don't go immediately for the previously sealed door. Instead, fight your way back to the entrance from the courtyard to find a Force surge secret. Then head through the doorway to the next area.

You now find yourself on a bridge. Defeat the Jedi that attack you and continue. Two turrets pop up from containers on the bridge's far edge. Either Force deflect their bolts back at them, or throw your lightsaber to destroy them.

Once both are scrap, you are rewarded with a saber crystal. Use this temporary power to quickly fight your way through the remaining Jedi on the bridge since they can't block your attacks. When you reach the door at the end of the bridge, wait for clone troopers to blast an opening for you.

Inside the next room are two double-bladed Jedi. At the back of the room are containers; throw these at them and then finish them off. You must also deal with a turret that descends from the ceiling. If that were not enough, two more of those tough Jedi show up to take you on. Use upgraded attacks to defeat them and continue through the doorway.

New Objective

- Use the turret to destroy Jedi starfighters

As soon as you enter the hangar, destroy the crate near the doorway to reveal a Force surge secret. Then take on the Jedi blocking your way to the area's other side.

At the hangar's far end is a turret. Climb onto it and use it to defeat several Jedi starfighters that rise up and shoot at you.

Press the Quick Slash button for quick fire. While the strong slash lets you fire a charged shot, this quickly overheats the turret and leaves you unable to fire while it cools down. Quick fire at each starfighter as it appears and only while it is under your reticule. Several quick bursts work better than sustained fire since it lets the turret cool a bit.

After you destroy all the starfighters, Anakin makes his way to the beacon and activates it, luring Jedi from all over back to the Jedi Temple—where he will destroy them.

Mission 12: The Final Lesson

Briefing

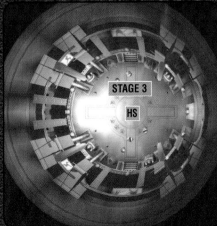

Jedi: Anakin Skywalker

Location: Coruscant

Secrets: 2

Despite Darth Vader's ferocity throughout the Temple, the Jedi refuse to go quietly. The harder the Jedi fight against him, the more convinced of their corruption and treachery the young Sith Lord becomes, which only fuels his anger and furthers his descent into the dark side.

Deep within the Jedi Temple, an incredibly skilled swordsman and Jedi Master named Cin Drallig prepares for Vader's coming. But before Cin can act, his most accomplished apprentice, Serra, confronts Vader on her own. With the fate of the Jedi Order at stake, these two Jedi are the Temple's last hope.

Objective
- Defeat Jedi Apprentice Serra

STAGE 1

SC

STAGE 2

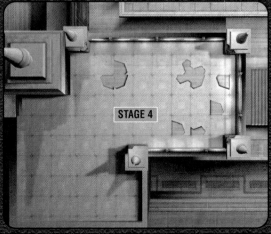

STAGE 3

HS

STAGE 4

LEGEND
FS *Force Surge*
SC *Saber Crystal*

Walkthrough

This mission is a double duel. You must defeat two Jedi, one at a time. First you take on the Jedi Apprentice. Serra has some powerful attacks and wields two lightsabers. There are several objects in the room that you can throw at Serra—even helmets.

> **TIP**
>
> Serra's attacks can be devastating. Therefore, always keep up a block because two lightsabers can really hurt.

One of the best tactics for this area is throwing Serra toward the electrical arcs at the rear of the room. You can knock off a big chunk of her health with this tactic, as well as Force grasping and pulling her toward you, and then delivering a couple quick slashes while she is airborne.

When Serra's health is down to half, she flees to another area. This room is a bit larger with nothing to throw and no electrical arcs. You must inflict all of the damage yourself this time.

Along the area's back are three hologram projectors. Destroy all three of them to reveal a saber crystal secret. This allows you to get in some good hits for a limited amount of time.

Serra has a powerful attack where she rushes right at you. If you see this coming, jump out of the way or prepare to get hurt. Stay in close to Serra to prevent her from using this attack. Keep up the pressure and you defeat this Jedi Apprentice.

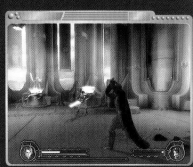

New Objective

• Defeat Jedi trainer Cin Drallig

Following the demise of Serra, you face Cin Dralling. This Jedi has some very powerful attacks and is tough to beat. Keep your lightsaber in a blocking posture during this part of the mission to keep his attacks from connecting.

> **TIP**
>
> Knock Cin Drallig to the ground, then use Force lightning on him when he's prone and helpless.

Cin Drallig's special attacks feature several quick slashes in succession. While each hit may not cause a lot of damage, quantity surely makes up for quality. However, if you are blocking, you can usually prevent most of the slashes from connecting with you.

MISSION 12: THE FINAL LESSON

Destroy the reddish pillar in the room's center to reveal a health surge secret.

As with Serra, throw Cin up into the air and then slash away. Use the many objects in the room to throw at the Jedi trainer as well. The shelves on the left and right sides contain many balls that you can Force throw at your opponent. Or you can throw Cin into objects for damage as well.

Fight defensively, shunting Cin's attacks and then moving in for your own while he is open. If you go in for an attack, use one of your special attacks to cause a lot of damage all at once.

When you have taken away half of Cin Drallig's health, the duel moves to an outdoor courtyard. This area features chunks from the floor and walls that you can throw at your opponent.

Cin really lets you have it here if you let down your guard. Stay defensive and avoid letting yourself get backed into a wall or corner where your maneuverability is severely reduced.

When Cin has depleted his Force meter, move in for the attack. He can't stun or push you away and is forced to block or use basic attacks. During this stage of the duel, Cin tries to Force heal. Do whatever you can to stop his attempts—throw your lightsaber or Force throw him while he is exposed.

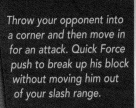

Throw your opponent into a corner and then move in for an attack. Quick Force push to break up his block without moving him out of your slash range.

Through determination and skill, you defeat Cin Drallig and claim another Jedi on your quest to destroy them all.

Mission 13: Attack of the Clones

Briefing

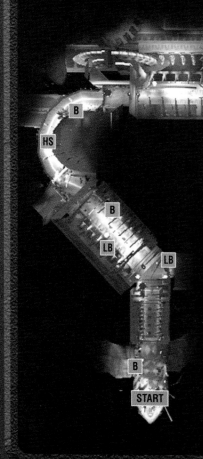

Jedi: Obi-Wan Kenobi

Location: Utapau

Secrets: 4

The Separatist armies on Utapau are beaten back, falling under the might of Obi-Wan Kenobi and his clone army. But Obi-Wan's victory is short-lived as Clone Commander Cody receives a secret coded message directly from Darth Sidious, implementing "Order 66"—a pre-programmed directive commanding the clones to turn on their Jedi leaders!

Suddenly under fire and running for his life, Obi-Wan must evade his former allies and find a way back to Coruscant.

Objective
- **Escape clone ambush**

LEGEND

B	Bacta Tank
FS	Force Surge
HS	Health Surge
LB	Large Bacta Tank
SC	Saber Crystal

Walkthrough

Unlike the previous missions on Utapau, you no longer have the assistance of the clone army. Instead, you are fighting them. However, Obi-Wan can now use the Jedi Mind Trick by pressing the Force Stun button. This causes a targeted clone trooper to begin fighting for you rather than against you. During this first part of the mission, you must fight off lots of clone troopers that rappel down onto the platform. They are tougher than battle droids and take a few slashes before going down. After you clear this platform, walk to the console and use it to lower the force field so you can continue.

TIP

Throughout this mission, you find several containers. Throw them at your enemies—especially at groups to take out several with one throw. Throw or destroy all of the containers as you progress through the mission since some are hiding bacta tanks.

As you head down this hallway, you see a turret and some droids, including a destroyer droid. Keep moving forward, but be ready to take on clone troopers that approach from behind you. Eliminate them, then continue toward the droids. Use the Force deflect ability to take out the destroyer droid and the turret. Also try throwing containers at these enemies to destroy them. Around the corner to the right, next to the door with the force field, is a large bacta tank. Cut through the panel to the large door's left and slash at the cables to open the door.

The next large corridor looks clear. However, as you get about halfway down, clone troopers rappel from the ceiling. In addition, battle droids come at you from behind. Use the Jedi Mind Trick on the clones so they temporarily help you fight off the battle droids—hen neutralize them before they turn on you again. As you destroy the containers in this area, you find a bacta tank and a large bacta tank.

New Objective

• **Defeat clone walkers**

You must now face a couple clone walkers. These enemies are tough since they shoot at you, and if they get in close, they step on you. You can't use the Jedi Mind Trick on them, but you can make them pause a bit by Force grasping the pilots. This gives you a second or two to get in and slash at the walkers. Focus on the legs with strong slashes and critical strikes. To avoid getting smashed, attack from the side and then jump out of the way when the walker turns toward you. If you keep the clone walker you are attacking between you and the second walker, you do not have to worry about it attacking you until the first is destroyed. If there are any containers left in this area, throw them at the walkers for some additional damage.

As you advance outside again along the walkway, you confront another clone walker. Use the same tactics as before. However, now you face another new foe—lone blaze troopers. These enemies fly around with jet packs and are armed with flamethrowers. They also like to grapple with you so they can throw you down and toast you. A quick Force push usually stuns them for a bit, allowing you to get in some slashes. Keep hitting the clone blaze troopers to prevent them from attacking you.

As you advance down the walkway, destroy containers along the right side to reveal a health surge secret, which should come in handy about now.

SECRET FOUND

New Objective

• **Use the Force to clear debris**

The walkway is blocked by debris. Walk to the designated point and use your Force powers to lift the blockage and clear your path.

At the walkway's end you face another clone walker. Force grasp the clone pilot to briefly halt the attack, and then move in with your own attack. A bacta tank is nearby. Now that the area here is clear, move to the indicated position and Force jump up onto a balcony.

On the balcony, you must fight off several clone blaze troopers. Since the area is small, keep slashing and attacking so they can't grapple and fry you. Defeat all of the enemies, then head to the door and cut your way through.

The next area can be dangerous. There is a console near where you begin that controls the door on the opposite side. However, the console is protected behind a force field. You must run across to the other side, taking out a couple battle droids along the way. Far away clone heavy gunners fire rockets at you while you are out in the open. Keep moving and they will not hit you. When you reach the other side, cut into a wall panel, then slash the cables to lower the shields. Run back to the console and use it. By now, clone troopers and blaze troopers have arrived. Stay to the left so you have some cover from the heavy gunners. Use Force powers to throw containers and clone troopers at the blaze troopers before they get in close. While you can stay to take them all out, another option is to run for the open door to advance into the next area and leave these clones behind.

TIP

To avoid dealing with the clone heavy gunners while taking on the other clones, neutralize them in advance. Before you run across to cut the wall panel, target the clone heavy gunners in the distance with your Force powers. Pick them up and pull them toward you, then drop them off the balcony. You can also throw them at each other. Just be ready to duck behind cover or jump out of the way of their rockets as you do this.

In the next room, immediately Force deflect against a turret on the wall. Also be ready for clone troopers to fire at you. As you move farther into the room, a destroyer droid and another turret start shooting. Move back toward where you entered and stun the destroyer droid, then take out the turret with either a saber throw or Force deflect. Slash at the four sections of power cable on the walls to shut down the force field blocking the console in the room's center.

Before you leave, throw your lightsaber at the large container on the far right side to reveal a Force surge secret. Destroying the large container in the room's middle yields a large bacta tank. With these two things, you are ready for the next challenging area. Use the console to open the large door to the right.

SECRET FOUND

New Objective

- **Defeat clone gunship**

This area is quite tough. You must take on a clone gunship single-handedly. In addition, there are several clone troopers that attack you. Go after the clone troopers first, while jumping out of the way of the laser blasts and missiles the clone gunship fires at you. Throw the containers at the troopers so you can focus on the gunship. A bacta tank is under one of the containers.

Use your lightsaber to destroy the clone gunship. While the enemy is not firing at you, Force target the gunship and then throw your lightsaber at it. Hold down the Saber Throw button to increase the range to ensure you get a hit. You can get in a couple quick throws before you must start moving to avoid taking damage. Keep up this tactic until you reduce the enemy's health to zero and destroy it. Don't try to Force deflect the clone gunship's attacks. It won't work.

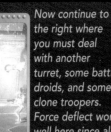

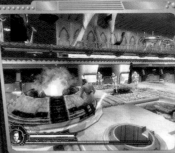

Now continue to the right where you must deal with another turret, some battle droids, and some clone troopers. Force deflect works well here since all of the attacks are coming from the same direction.

To make his escape, Obi-Wan jumps down onto a clone juggernaut. To complete your final objective, destroy the juggernaut's two turrets. One is located to the left; go after it with some basic slashes. Before you can concentrate on the second turret to the right, fight off lots of clone troopers. After clearing off a group, move to the right and throw your lightsaber at the turret to damage it from a safe distance. Then go after another group of troopers before returning to take another throw. Repeat this until the turret is destroyed and Obi-Wan can escape from Utapau.

SECRET FOUND: SABER CRYSTAL

Destroy the container in the far right corner to reveal a saber crystal secret. After you have it, cut through the locked door to move on to the next area.

SECRET FOUND: HEALTH SURGE: MAX HEALTH INCREASED

Clear out the next room, which includes destroyer droids and battle droids. Destroy the large container next to the wall panel to receive a health surge secret. Then cut through the panel and slash at the cables to shut down the force field blocking your way.

In the next room is a destroyer droid, some battle droids, and clone troopers. Start by using the Jedi Mind Trick on a few of the troopers to let them fight for you. Then stun the destroyer droid to lower its shields and move in for the kill. Eliminate all enemies here to continue.

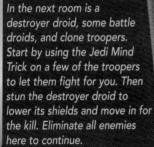

New Objective

- Disable clone juggernaut defenses

Mission 14: Assassination on Mustafar

Briefing

Jedi: Anakin Skywalker

Location: Separatist Cruiser

Secrets: 5

On Coruscant, the Jedi Order is broken and the Temple in ruins. With no one left to oppose him, Darth Sidious ready to declare the Clone Wars over and appoint him: emperor of the galaxy. The only matter left to attend to the remaining Separatist leaders, who are hiding in the Mustafar system. Sidious dispatches Darth Vader to the volcanic world to end their lives with a final betrayal.

LEGEND

- **B** Bacta Tank
- **FS** Force Surge
- **HS** Health Surge
- **LB** Large Bacta Tank
- **SC** Saber Crystal

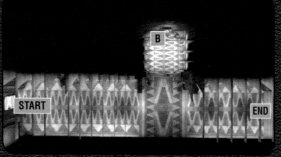

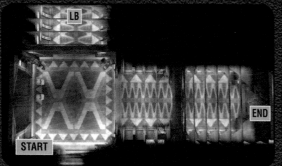

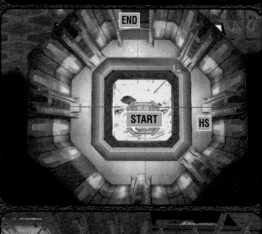

Objective

- Assassinate Separatist leaders

Walkthrough

You must cover a lot of ground in this mission and take on hordes of enemies. Just think of all the experience you will earn! The first enemies you face are the Neimoidian guards. They are armed with a shock baton that can temporarily stun you if it hits. Therefore, use Force powers to keep them away, throw your lightsaber at them, or go on the offensive and get in a combo against them before they can get in an attack of their own.

There is a secret in the first area of this mission. Destroy the large container to receive a Force surge.

SECRET FOUND

New Objective

- Use the Force to move magma hover platform

A magma hover platform blocks your path. Move to the designated area and then press the Force button to clear your way. Continue on, taking out some more Neimoidian guards. When you reach the locked door, cut your way through.

Pass through a corridor to face a few Neimoidian guards. Eliminate them and then head for the corridor's end, where a turret and some destroyer droids await. Force deflect the turret's shots to take it out, then use Force lightning to stun the destroyer droid so you can finish it off with lightsaber slashes. Use the console to open the door.

In this next area, you get your first experience with a Neimoidian brute. Concentrate on him first since he can cause the most damage. However, you must also slash out at the Neimoidian guards that try to sneak up on you from behind. There are also some Neimoidian scouts on the parallel conveyor belt at a distance. Armed with sniper rifles, they shoot at you while you are fighting. Get rid of them as soon as possible by targeting them and using the Force to pull them toward you (just enough to get them off their conveyor belt), then drop them in the magma below. After you clear off your conveyor belt, Force jump to the far belt and take on a destroyer droid. Pick up the nearby bacta tank and then get ready for another Neimoidian brute and some guards. After they are dead, continue to the left.

TIP

Neimoidian brutes block regular slashes and combos, so use the Force to pick them up and throw them. Try Force grasping and pulling them toward yourself, and then slash at them while they are in the air and defenseless. Repeating this a couple times finishes off the toughest of the brutes. In some areas, you can even throw enemies off of the conveyor belts with the Force so you don't even have to use the lightsaber.

The next area offers a few Neimoidian guards. They are quick work, but a couple Neimoidian brutes then come at you, one after another. Throw and slash to defeat them, then burn your way through the locked door and advance to the next area.

New Objective

- Lift magma gun

Head left to take on a brute and more guards until you reach a position across from a platform protected by a couple turrets and some battle droids. Force deflect the turret shots to take them out and then throw the battle droids at each other or off the platform to clear it. Force jump across to the platform.

You must take on a few more battle droids here. Then enter the room and use the console to lift the magma gun blocking the conveyor belt. Pick up the large bacta tank while you are there.

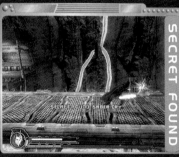

SECRET FOUND

Force jump back to the conveyor. However, instead of continuing left, backtrack to the right to earn a saber crystal secret. Quickly head back to the left so you can maximize the abilities of this secret.

As you advance to the left, a couple Neimoidian scouts shoot at another magma gun, dropping it right in your path. Use the Force to knock them off their platform, then Force jump across. Quickly move into the small room and take out the power cables on the left to destroy a turret that appears outside. Then engage any Neimoidians that come out to attack. When it is clear, head out and to the left so you can Force jump back to the conveyor belt.

Back on the belt, get ready to use Force lightning to stun a couple destroyer droids and then neutralize them. As you continue, a hover platform drops off some Neimoidian guards and a brute. Run to the right so you can avoid the fire of a Neimoidian scout. To quickly get rid of a group of Neimoidian guards coming at you, throw one of the guards at the rest of the group and then throw each of them off the conveyor belt. Or you can mix it up with the lightsaber. Then go after the scout with Force lightning or a Force throw. Having cleared the opposite platform, Force jump across, pick up a bacta tank to the left, and then cut your way through a locked door.

You are once again indoors, so no throwing enemies off into the magma. As you advance to the right, take out groups of battle droids until you reach a force field. Eliminate the two Neimoidian brutes there, then head back to the left where you must take on a couple more. Defeat them, then cut the power cable to disable the force field. Pick up the bacta tank and head back to the right.

SECRET FOUND

Three containers block your path. Destroy the one on the right to earn a saber crystal. Quickly move forward, taking out the battle droids in your way and the Neimoidian scout at the walkway's end. When you reach the end, a couple destroyer droids come out to greet you. Throw a container at them and then move in to finish them off as well as any other enemies that come at you. A large bacta tank is also here.

Now head to the right until you come to another force field. To disable it, slash at the power cables on either side of the door. Kill the Neimoidian brute on the other side, then use the console to open another door.

TIP

You cannot block the shots of Neimoidian scouts with Force deflect. Therefore, since all other Neimoidians have only close-range attacks, target scouts first (if possible). Try to take them out with a quick Force throw. If you can't do that, at least find some cover or move out of the scout's line of fire while you deal with closer enemies.

New Objective

• Disable force field

You come to a gap with magma down below. There is a Neimoidian scout on the platform across from you. Before he can get off a shot, use the Force to throw him off the platform. Then use the console to extend a walkway so you can cross to the platform.

New Objective

• Access magma lift controls

As you move across, you face a couple Neimoidian brutes with another scout on a different platform. Quickly throw the brutes into the magma and take up a position behind the metal barrier so the scout can't hit you. Use the Force to throw the scout off the platform, then target the power cables by where the second scout was standing. This lowers the barrier so you can access the controls to the magma lift.

When the lift reaches the top, prepare for an attack by two Neimoidian brutes, two guards, and a turret. Throw the guards off as soon as possible, Force deflect the turret's bolts to destroy it, then deal with the brutes.

SECRET FOUND

Before continuing, move over to the force field on the left. Use the Force to throw a container on the other side at a power cable. This lowers the force field and allows you to get a Force surge secret.

SECRET FOUND

After Anakin heads up to the next level, move back into the lift area and make your way around to the right. Get rid of a container to earn a health surge secret.

SECRET FOUND: HEALTH SURGE. MAX HEALTH INCREAS

Now return to the large room and head left, taking on Neimoidians and a couple destroyer droids along the way. You then enter a control room where you must deal with Neimoidian guards and a few Neimoidian brutes. Toss them around and slice them up, then continue after the Separatist leaders. You are getting close.

Once in the meeting room, assassinate all of the leaders left behind by Nute Gunray, the head Neimoidian leader, as he tries to escape. This is easy since the Neimoidians do not put up any fight at all.

New Objective

• Destroy Nute Gunray in Neimoidian shuttle

The last stage of this mission is very similar to Obi-Wan's experience with the clone gunship in the previous mission. Anakin must dodge fire from the shuttle and take out Neimoidian guards, while throwing his lightsaber at the shuttle. Keep moving and throw whenever you have a chance.

When the shuttle takes enough damage, it crashes into the magma. Anakin, the new Sith Lord, has completed yet another of his master's tasks.

Mission 15: Aftermath in the Temple

Briefing

Jedi: Obi-Wan Kenobi

Location: Coruscant

Secrets: 6

Objective
- Shut down Temple beacon

Walkthrough

After surviving Order 66, Obi-Wan Kenobi endeavors to prevent the Jedi Order's devastation. Reunited with Yoda aboard Senator Bail Organa's personal starship, the Jedi plan a return to Coruscant, hoping to find clues to their mysterious and dire situation within the Jedi Temple.

Obi-Wan enters the Temple, which is in ruins after Darth Vader's attack on the Jedi. While Vader has left on an assignment for Darth Sidious, he has left behind an army of clones. You have Yoda to help you fight.

LEGEND

B	Bacta Tank
FS	Force Surge
HS	Health Surge
LB	Large Bacta Tank
SC	Saber Crystal

Start off by engaging the clones. Go after the clone heavy gunners first, since their weapons cause you more damage. The clones tend to form groups, so a single slash can hit more than one enemy at a time. Use a saber throw to take out the clone on top of the rubble in the area's middle. Clones continue to drop down or climb up onto the level where you are fighting, so be ready for them. After you clear this area, Force jump to the upper walkway. Walk left a bit to find a small bacta tank.

TIP

When dealing with lots of clones, use your Force powers. The Jedi Mind Trick forces clone troopers to temporarily fight for you. Also use the Force to pick up and throw a trooper at another trooper to take out two of your enemies with one sweep of your hand.

Take on more clone troopers and heavy gunners here. There is less room to maneuver here, and the enemy comes at you from both sides. Therefore, you must fight in two directions to prevent getting attacked from behind. At this walkway's end is another bacta tank.

The clones detonate an explosive, causing a large column to fall. This provides Obi-Wan and Yoda a bridge across to this room's other side. Fight your way up onto the walkway and destroy the container near the column. You are rewarded with a saber crystal.

Fight your way along the walkway, heading right. In addition to the clones you have been fighting, clone blaze troopers now attack you. However, after getting the saber crystal, you will be tough to stop and will rack up experience as quickly as possible.

When you near the walkway's end, you find an alcove with large and small containers. Destroy the small container on the left to reveal a Force surge secret.

You are on your own in the next area in which you fight; Yoda has moved off in a different direction. Destroy some containers to uncover a couple large bacta tanks, then start going after the clones. Again, a lot of them come at you. After you clear out most of the troopers and heavy gunners, clone blaze troopers come at you one or two at a time. Keep slashing at them, and they can't get in an attack. A Force push also makes them pause as they are preparing to attack. Neutralize all of the clones that come at you. Then jump onto the middle rubble and Force jump to the next area.

After you arrive and regain control of Obi-Wan, quickly throw the rock in the upper left corner to reveal a saber crystal. You want this at the start so every clone you eliminate for a limited amount of time gives you the maximum amount of experience possible. As before, you face troopers, heavy gunners, and blaze troopers here.

New Objective

- Aid Yoda in moving debris

After you clear this area, Yoda asks for your help in moving a large piece of rubble. Move to the designated position and press the Force push button to move the obstacle.

Jump down to another walkway and destroy the large container off to the right to reveal a health surge secret. Continue to the walkway's end and turn to the right. A couple of turrets pop out of the wall, so get ready to Force deflect their bolts back at them. You can also take out both with a single well-thrown lightsaber. Target one and as the lightsaber circles around, it destroys the second turret on its way back to you. Burn your way through the door with your lightsaber.

New Objective

- Defeat library security protocol

The next room is the Jedi library. Here you must take on lots of clones with the help of Yoda. There are several objects that you can throw, and because of the close quarters, you can often attack more than one enemy at a time with quick slashes. If you have some area attacks, this is a great place to use them. After you clear the library's lower floor, Force jump to the balcony on the second level.

When you reach the top, instead of following Yoda to the left, head to the right and take out a single clone trooper. Pick up the stone head on the ground to find a saber crystal.

Now head to the left and help Yoda take on some more clones. Expect some clone blaze troopers here as well. Defeat them, then continue to the wall panel and cut it open. Slash at the power cables to shut down the force field at this area's far right end, near where you found the secret. Then move to the door, taking out any clones that stand in your way. Cut through the locked door with your lightsaber to enter the next area.

You are now at one end of a long corridor. Advance to the right and be ready for all types of clones. As usual, concentrate on the clone blaze troopers when they appear since they are the biggest threat to your health. With a considerable amount of room to maneuver, use saber throws and Force pushes or throws to attack enemies at a distance, thinning them out before you close.

TIP

If you have upgraded some dash attacks, this corridor is long enough to put them to use, allowing you to plow through several enemies at once, eliminating or heavily damaging them in the process.

As you fight down this corridor, you eventually come across a health surge secret along the far wall. Pick it up to restore your health to its maximum amount.

New Objective

- Defeat clone gunships
- Use turret to defeat clone gunships

You must now take on a couple clone gunships. Unlike the last time Obi-Wan had to do this, he now has some heavy fire power. When you get your new orders, immediately climb on the turret at the corridor's end. As with other turrets you have used, the Quick Slash button fires fast shots while the Strong Slash button fires charged shots. Stick with the quick shots as you take on the enemy. The gunships fire missiles at you, so after getting in a couple hits on the gunships, shoot down the missiles with quick shots before they hit and damage you. Fire only when a gunship or missile is in your sights so you don't overheat the turret. After you destroy both clone gunships, Obi-Wan climbs down and heads toward the beacon.

The final area of this mission introduces you to the last new enemy: clone assassins. These enemies are incredibly fast and armed with vibroblades built into their armor. Because of their speed, these assassins are difficult to hit. Try to use area attacks, especially when there is more than one assassin near you. Then keep up the pressure with quick slashes and combos. Try not to let more than one get in close at a time or you will have trouble. The best defense against the assassins is to maintain the offense, so your lightsaber is in constant motion, preventing them from getting in a hit on you. After you eliminate a couple of groups of clone assassins, the way to the beacon is clear and Obi-Wan can complete his mission.

Mission 16: A Friendship in Flames

Briefing

Jedi: Obi-Wan Kenobi

Location: Mustafar

Secrets: 0

Objective
- **Defeat Darth Vader**

Learning of Anakin's descent into the darkness while inside the Jedi Temple, Obi-Wan travels to Mustafar for a final confrontation with his old friend and former Padawan.

STAGE 1

STAGE 2

STAGE 3

STAGE 4

STAGE 5

STAGE 6

Walkthrough

For this mission, you get to recreate the epic, climactic duel from the movie as Obi-Wan and Anakin fight each other with all of the Jedi powers at their disposal. As with all duels, keep up your lightsaber to block your opponent's attacks.

TIP

This mission has no secrets or bacta tanks. The only way to restore your health is to Force heal yourself.

Start off with some of your more powerful attacks that you have gained through upgrading. Your Force meter is full, so you have Force to spare. This also lets you put the hurt on Anakin early in the duel as you take the initiative.

Anakin is good about blocking—Obi-Wan taught him well. Therefore, Force throw him up in the air toward you, then slash away. You can usually get in at least two or three hits each time.

TIP

This duel can be a bit confusing at times when the action is intense, since you may momentarily forget which Jedi you are controlling. You have dueled with each in previous missions and it is easy to start focusing on the opposite character. To overcome this, pay close attention to your character's actions and follow your own lightsaber rather than that of your opponent.

After you have reduced Anakin's health by a quarter, the duel moves indoors into the Mustafar control room. While there are no objects to throw, the holographic tables in the middle of the room provide obstacles around which you must fight.

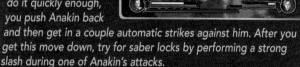

As both Jedi simultaneously attack with a strong slash, they lock sabers. When this happens, press the two Slash buttons—Quick and Strong—together as fast as you can. If you do it quickly enough, you push Anakin back and then get in a couple automatic strikes against him. After you get this move down, try for saber locks by performing a strong slash during one of Anakin's attacks.

Maintain the initiative as much as possible. Stay at a distance until you want to attack, so Anakin can't attack you. Then either use the Force to throw him into the air and break his blocking, or use a powerful attack combo with the Force.

As you continue to wound Anakin, the duel moves to the third location, which is a bit more open than the control room. There are a few objects you can throw here.

Remember to shunt Anakin's attacks, blocking with your lightsaber and then going on the offensive at the end of his combo. This usually lets you get in the first hit of a combo, opening up Anakin for the remaining slashes.

The duel's fourth stage is even more open. This lets you use your dash attacks. There are also many containers around. Since they tend to get destroyed when two lightsabers are slashing about, pick them up at the start of this area and throw them at Anakin. Try to hit him with a container when he is just starting an attack.

The next stage takes place on a narrow walkway suspended over the magma. You have a lot of linear maneuverability, but not much side to side. Therefore, you can't effectively jump to the side to avoid dash attacks—and neither can your opponent.

If you need more health, jump away and Force heal. When Anakin comes after you, block, get in a hit or two, then jump away to Force heal again.

TIP

Get your health as high as possible during the fifth stage on the narrow walkway. The distance you can put between Anakin and yourself gives you time to effectively Force heal. The next stage will not allow for such a luxury.

The duel's final stage takes place on a very small platform floating above the magma. No matter where you are, you are always in range for an attack, so always be in a blocking stance.

Grapple attacks work well here since you are almost always right next to your opponent. In addition, when you throw Anakin, he will land close enough for you to get in a quick slash while he is down.

Advanced attacks almost always connect with your opponent in this tiny area. Just watch your Force meter. You always want to keep it at least a third full so you can quickly throw your lightsaber if Anakin tries to Force heal himself.

After you have taken away all of Anakin's health, the duel ends with Obi-Wan as the victor.

Mission 17: Revenge of the Sith

Briefing

Jedi: Anakin Skywalker

Location: Mustafar

Secrets: 0

Objective
- Defeat Obi-Wan Kenobi

With the Separatist leaders on Mustafar now eliminated, Darth Vader prepares to return to Coruscant only to find his former friend and master, Obi-Wan Kenobi, waiting for him. Accusations fly between the two, and it becomes clear to the young Sith Lord that Palpatine was right: Obi-Wan, too, has been tainted by the Jedi's corruption and must also be destroyed.

Walkthrough

This duel is essentially identical to the previous mission. However, this time you play as Anakin (Sith Lord Darth Vader).

STAGE 1

STAGE 3

STAGE 5

STAGE 2

STAGE 4

STAGE 6

Anakin has some different advanced attacks than Obi-Wan Kenobi. Therefore, you must fight differently. Obi-Wan is a much tougher opponent, so be really careful and fight defensively.

TIP

As always, use the environment to your benefit. Throw objects and try to corner your opponent so that Force push will stun Obi-Wan rather than push him out of slashing range.

This duel progresses through the same six stages, so by now, they should all be very familiar. In the control room, get in close and grapple with your opponent. Then when you throw or knock him away, there is usually a wall or table that halts Obi-Wan's movement, allowing you to move in for a slash.

Advanced attacks work great while you have a lot of Force power built up, since these attacks cannot be blocked.

Obi-Wan can easily block Anakin's Force lightning attack while Obi-Wan is up and fighting. However, once you throw him down, he is wide open for a shocking assault.

By this time, you should have mastered the saber lock. Therefore, whenever one occurs, use it to get in a good strike against Obi-Wan.

While this platform has no walls, neither of you can fall off. Therefore, throwing Obi-Wan toward the edge is just like throwing him at a wall—he stops at the edge and then drops, giving you a chance to hit him while he is still in the air and won't move away from you.

By the mid part of the duel, Obi-Wan begins to Force heal. It is vital that you do not let him do this or at least cut his healing short. He can heal quite quickly, so stop it with a saber throw, attack, or even a Force push. While healing, Obi-Wan cannot block.

The final stage against Obi-Wan is very difficult. He is a bit tougher in close and is good at using advanced attacks. While a powerful attack of your own can do some damage, you are usually better off saving your Force for picking up your opponent and then using basic combos to attack. Again, keep some Force on the meter to attack when Obi-Wan tries to heal.

Try to get Obi-Wan into a situation where you can use your strengths. Whether it's a saber lock, Force throws, or certain combos and attacks, the key at this point in the duel is to cause damage to your opponent while minimizing the damage you take.

Use everything you have learned up to this point against Obi-Wan and you will defeat your old master. You will also rewrite history.

Bonus Mission 1: The General's Protectors

Briefing

Character: Grievous' Bodyguard

Location: Utapau

General Grievous' bodyguards are the deadliest of droids, as the attacking clone army quickly discovers.

Objective
• Defeat clone troopers

Walkthrough

While you got to fight against these tough droids during the story missions, in this bonus mission, you actually get to fight as one of Grievous' bodyguards. Getting used to the way they fight takes some practice. However, these droids are very effective at engaging multiple enemies at the same time.

As you move around the area, you notice that the Grievous' bodyguard walks quite slow, allowing the enemy to shoot at you as you approach. The key is not to walk, but to slide about the area. To do this, hold down the Block button and move the left analog stick in the direction you want to move. While doing this, also press the Jump button. While sliding, you can move the analog stick to turn and even slide around an opponent.

NOTE

There are several bacta tanks and large bacta tanks scattered about the area. You find them when you destroy any of the consoles in this area.

78

Grievous' bodyguard has a long continuous combo. Once started, you cannot stop it. This allows you to keep hitting an enemy over and over with your electrified battle staff. However, it also commits you to attacking in one direction for a couple seconds. Therefore, make sure there is an enemy in front of you when you begin your attack.

At the beginning, you face only clone troopers. However, after a bit, some clone heavy gunners appear. Since they can cause you a lot of damage, slide toward them and take them out as quickly as possible.

TIP

At the mission's beginning, you have another of Grievous' bodyguards fighting with you. While standing next to your twin, press the Quick and Strong Slash buttons simultaneously, as if to grapple. This sets up an attack where the two bodyguards work together. Use this early since the other bodyguard is destroyed by mid-mission—especially if you don't stay in close for mutual support.

Eventually, you must face clone blaze troopers. To beat them, get in close and keep that staff spinning. Because of the staff's length and the spinning slashes, you can actually get hits on several blaze troopers as they surround you and try to get in a grapple. If they ever move away from you, slide back toward them or toward a bacta tank if you need one.

New Objective
• Defeat crab droid

Just as you defeat the last clone blaze trooper, you must take on a crab droid. If your health is lacking, quickly slide to pick up some bacta tanks that may still be around. Then move in to attack the crab droid.

Unlike the missions where you had to fight the crab droids while playing as a Jedi, as Grievous' bodyguard, you cannot jump onto the droid's back since the bodyguard cannot grapple. However, this time, your battle staff is sufficient to attack it from the ground. Watch out for its laser blasts, jumping or sliding out of the way. Quickly move in for a couple strikes, then slide away before the crab droid hits you with its claws. Repeat this tactic until you reduce its health to zero, completing this first bonus mission.

Bonus Mission 2: Grievous on the Run

Briefing

Character: General Grievous

Location: Utapau

TIP
As you move around the area, jump toward your enemies rather than walk. This makes it harder for the enemy to shoot at you, and you actually move quicker with a leap than on foot.

Seeing his plans of conquest on Utapau unravel before him, Grievous flees toward his hidden starship, cutting down any clone trooper foolish enough to stand in his way.

Objective
- Destroy the clone troopers and the droids

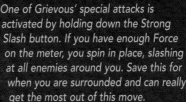

One of Grievous' special attacks is activated by holding down the Strong Slash button. If you have enough Force on the meter, you spin in place, slashing at all enemies around you. Save this for when you are surrounded and can really get the most out of this move.

If two lightsabers are not enough, press the Saber Throw button and General Grievous brings out two more lightsabers for a total of four! This causes a drain on your Force meter; when you run out of Force, the two extra lightsabers are stowed once again. Save this, and Force, for when you have several enemies that you must deal with quickly.

It is important to keep moving during this mission. All of your enemies can shoot at you from a distance. Since this area is not very big, you are like a fish in a barrel. Furthermore, there are few bacta tanks in this area and you cannot Force heal. When you lose health, there are few chances to regain it.

Walkthrough

While you can play as General Grievous in the multiplayer duels, this bonus mission lets you try your fighting skills against several enemies of various levels of difficulty.

Grievous is somewhat slow, and many of his combos are somewhat long. However, with two lightsabers, you are sure to destroy whatever you go after.

You have some new attacks at your disposal with General Grievous. Press the Force Push button and your character pulls out a blaster and shoots. This gives you a ranged attack somewhat like a Jedi's saber throw.

Toward the mission's end, you take on Obi-Wan Kenobi. Keep up your guard and follow through with combos when you see an opening. Obi-Wan is vulnerable to Grievous's powerful grapple and unblockable special attacks. Wear down the Jedi, then switch to four lightsabers to deal maximum damage. Defeat Obi-Wan to complete the bonus mission.

Bonus Mission 3: Mustafar Lava Challenge

Briefing

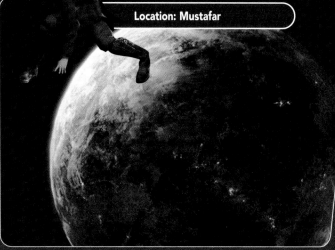

Jedi: Anakin Skywalker

Location: Mustafar

On his mission to silence the Separatist leaders, Darth Vader must navigate Mustafar's constantly moving platform system in order to reach his prey.

Objective
- **Navigate lava processing trench**

Walkthrough

BE CAREFUL NOT TO FALL INTO THE DEADLY LAVA BELOW!

This bonus mission is more like one of the story missions. However, unlike those missions, here you can actually fall off the platforms and walkways. Falling into the lava ends the mission, so avoid this. To begin, you must jump from one platform to the next.

The third platform moves up and down and allows you to access an upper walkway where you take on battle droids and Neimoidian guards. However, to avoid this fight, drop down to the lower walkway and head to a point from where you can Force jump onto some pipes. To the right is a bacta tank and some power cables. Slash at the cables to raise a walkway off to the left so you can continue.

> **TIP**
> Whenever you get a break from being attacked, Force heal yourself. Other than the bacta tank by the power cables, there are no more in this mission. Therefore, you must heal yourself.

Continue to the left and around on the walkway. Some Neimoidian scouts come at you and fire with their long-range rifles. Either throw containers at them or pick them up with the Force and throw them into the lava.

Move to the console and use it to activate the elevator platform. Quickly move to the left onto the platform and ride it to the upper level. When you reach the top, jump over to the walkway and begin taking out the battle droids that come at you from the left and the right.

You must also worry about battle droids that shoot at you on the next walkway. Use the Force to pull them toward you, dropping them into the lava; or throw a battle droid into another one to take out two with one throw. After you eliminate all of the battle droids on your walkway, throw your lightsaber up at the power cables on both the left and right sides to cause a couple narrow platforms to appear in between the two walkways. Jump across to the platform, and then onto the walkway.

At this mission's final area, you must fight battle droids and Neimoidian guards. Before you jump from the second moving platform to the structure, use your Force powers to throw as many enemies into the lava as possible. Then, when you make your move, you are better able to take on the two turrets that descend from the ceiling. Either use Force deflect or throw your lightsaber at the turrets to destroy them.

As you reach the walkway, a couple Neimoidian brutes climb up to come after you. Be careful because a solid hit from one of these guys might push you into the lava below. Use the Force to either throw these enemies into the lava or to pick them up so you can slash at them without them being able to block. Force heal and then let your Force build up before continuing.

Continue fighting off all the enemies that come at you. After you eliminate them, the mission is complete.

Jump over to the edge of the pipes, and then onto the first moving platform. You must time it just right to jump to the second platform, because both are moving up and down.

New Objective

- Defeat Neimoidian opposition

Bonus Mission 4: Size Matters Not

Briefing

Character: Yoda

Location: Coruscant

The clone troopers have betrayed the Jedi and have overtaken the Temple. Searching the Temple's ruins and separated from Obi-Wan Kenobi, Yoda faces an almost overwhelming wave of clone soldiers.

Objective
• Defeat clone troopers

Walkthrough

You finally get a chance to take control of one of the most powerful Jedi Masters—Yoda. While he is small, this wizened old Jedi is one tough fighter. Those clone troopers don't know what they are in for.

When large groups of enemies come at you, use the Force push. Yoda has a much stronger push than other Jedi, allowing him to push several enemies at once. The power of this push alone eliminates clone troopers.

Since the clone troopers have rifles, move in close and let loose with a whirlwind of slashes. Yoda's speed and small size make it difficult for enemies to get a hit on him while he is in motion and on the attack. Target clone heavy gunners first since a single hit from them causes you some serious damage.

Whenever you get a lull, use it to Force heal yourself. Keep your health meter at least half full at all times.

About halfway through the fight, clone blaze troopers arrive. These are actually a bit easier for Yoda to deal with since they must get in close to attack. Keep Yoda on the offensive and the blaze troopers have trouble getting a grip on the Jedi.

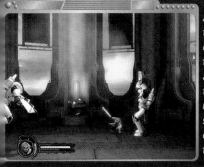

After you eliminate the first group of clone blaze troopers, more arrive. Quickly move to attack them and maintain the initiative so they don't have a chance to counterattack.

New Objective

- Defeat clone assassins

The clones have saved their best for last. You have already taken on clone assassins while playing as Obi-Wan. However, now you must defeat five at once. Start off with a Force push that damages most if not all of the assassins. Then approach one and start attacking.

Luckily, at first Yoda faces only one or two assassins at a time. As you attack, they quickly dodge and move away. Keep up the attacks, never stopping, and you will get in a hit every now and then. As long as you keep the assassins moving to avoid you, they can't go after you.

Use the Force push whenever you can target a group of assassins and have enough Force on your meter. Using this attack while slashing away at an individual actually causes enough damage to some of the bystanders that you defeat them without needing to use the lightsaber on them.

Stick with your quick slashes, because you will have a hard time hitting an assassin with a slower but more powerful attack. Focus on one assassin at a time to slowly whittle down the group. More appear, so keep using the same tactics.

Force heal as needed, jumping away from the assassins for a brief respite, then getting back into the fray. After you defeat all the clone assassins, the mission is complete.

Bonus Mission 5: Episode IV Death Star

Briefing

> Character: Darth Vader

> Location: Death Star

After many years, Darth Vader and Ben Kenobi come face-to-face once more. By engaging Darth Vader in combat, Ben Kenobi allows Luke Skywalker to escape certain death... but at what cost?

Objective
• Defeat Ben Kenobi

Walkthrough

For over a quarter century, fans have been waiting to take part in the classic duel between Darth Vader and Ben Kenobi. Here is your chance.

As with all duels, keep up your lightsaber to block Ben's attacks against you, and look for opportunities to get in hits of your own.

When a saber lock occurs, rapidly and simultaneously press on the Quick and Strong Slash buttons. You avoid taking damage from Ben's attack, and you can get in some hits of your own against your former master.

TIP

If you can get in close, Darth Vader's grapple attack is actually a Force Choke. Just simultaneously hold down the Quick and Strong Slash buttons to pick up Ben Kenobi and choke the health out of him.

Ben Kenobi has some tricks up his sleeves. Watch out for his Force stun. Block it with a Force push or you just stand there, waiting for your opponent to get a free attack on you.

If possible, back up Ben against a wall so you can give a quick Force push to drop his block, followed by a combo of slashes.

Even out in the middle, you can use the Force to break Kenobi's blocks. If you can time it just right, pull him toward you and then slash away. These slashes can keep your opponent up in the air where he is defenseless against your assault.

By the duel's middle, Ben is down to half of his strength; stay in close and keep the pressure on so he can't Force heal himself. Keep slashing, even though Ben blocks, and you eventually get in a hit. When he goes on the attack, block and shunt his blows, so you can counterattack with slashes of your own.

Ben tries to push you back with the Force, giving him an opportunity to Force heal. If this happens, throw your lightsaber to halt the healing and instead cause some damage.

Continue on the offensive, throwing Ben about the area and looking for openings or creating them yourself, and you will defeat Ben Kenobi—the Jedi who has eluded you for these many years.

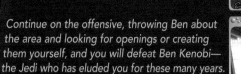

www.lucasarts.com/eps

Multiplayer Duelists

Now you can take on the role of nine different duelists—each with their own special attacks and abilities. At the game's beginning, you can duel only with Anakin and Obi-Wan. As you progress through the single-player story missions, you unlock the remaining seven duelists.

Let's look at each of these nine duelists and how best to fight as each. While most of the duelists share the same basic controls, each also has four special attacks—many of which are quite powerful and may require Force from your meter in order to execute.

Basic Controls for All Characters

Name	Xbox	PS2
Run	→	Left analog ⇨
Jump	Ⓐ	✕
Fast slash	Ⓧ	■
Strong slash	Ⓨ	▲
Critical strike	Ⓑ	●
Block	Ⓛ	L1

Anakin Skywalker

Anakin Skywalker is a powerful Jedi. He has many impressive moves and fights in the duels with his Dark Jedi powers. All of his special attacks require the Force and are stand-alone attacks. Use regular combos and blocks to fight your opponent while you build up Force power to execute the special attacks and other actions requiring Force.

Anakin's Fury Whirlwind attack uses Force power and allows Anakin to attack all enemies within a 360-degree radius. This attack cannot be blocked and can also allow for another attack with regular slashes before the opponent can block.

With the Fury Explosion, Anakin uses the Force to cause damage to nearby opponents.

Fury Corkscrew is a dash attack allowing Anakin to engage an opponent while starting at a distance. It causes damage to the target, and it knocks down the opponent, providing an opportunity for follow-up attacks.

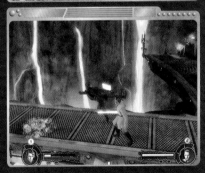

When Anakin uses the Fury Sai Bomb, he executes a combination slashing attack that concludes with a high, sweeping kick. You must be close to and facing the opponent or your kick may miss. When it connects, it causes additional damage and a short stun.

COMBAT CHARTS

Basic Controls

Name	Xbox	PS2
Saber throw	WHT	L2
Force push/grasp	Ⓡ	R1
Target select	Ⓡ	Right analog
Strafe	Hold Ⓛ+→	Hold L1 + Left analog ⇨
Force lightning	Ⓛ	R2
Force heal	Click Ⓛ+Ⓡ	Click left analog + right analog
Force speed	→,→	Left analog ⇨, left analog ⇨

Special Attacks

Name	Xbox	PS2
Fury Whirlwind	→ + hold Ⓨ	Left analog ⇨ + hold ▲
Fury Explosion	Hold Ⓨ	Hold ▲
Fury Corkscrew	→+ hold Ⓧ	Left analog ⇨+ hold ■
Fury Sai Bomb	Ⓐ+hold Ⓨ	✕+hold ▲

Obi-Wan Kenobi

Obi-Wan is a powerful Jedi who stays on the light side of the Force. While proficient at actions such as Force push and stun, his special attacks can also be devastating. All four attacks use the Force and allow Obi-Wan to put the hurt on his opponents.

For a medium-range attack, use the Focus Shockwave. It features a powerful Force assault on your opponent that causes damage and a short stun effect.

The Focus Slash Combo is a fast series of slashes augmented by the speed and power of the Force. It can only be used when your opponent is close.

The Focus Lunge Strike is a dash attack that damages your opponents and knocks them down. Follow up this attack with additional slashes.

For an attack featuring a flying kick, use the Focus Sai Bomb. Make sure you are moving directly toward your opponent, or you may fly right past without causing any damage at all.

COMBAT CHARTS

Basic Controls

Name	Xbox	PS2
Saber throw	WHT	L2
Force push/grasp	R	R1
Target select	R	Right analog
Strafe	Hold L+→	Hold L1 + Left analog →
Force stun	L	R2
Force heal	Click L+R	Click left analog + right analog
Force speed	→,→	Left analog →, left analog →

Special Attacks

Name	Xbox	PS2
Focus Shockwave	Hold →+Y	Hold Left analog → + ▲
Focus Slash Combo	Hold Y	Hold ▲
Focus Lunge Strike	Hold →+X	Hold Left analog → + ■
Focus Sai Bomb	A+hold Y	X+hold ▲

Count Dooku

Count Dooku's fighting style reflects an older style of Jedi lightsaber dueling similar to fencing. His basic slashes are short and more directed toward the target rather than including spinning and wide slashes. Having turned to the dark side, Count Dooku's Force powers focus on damaging attacks rather than stun attacks.

The Force Lightning Explosion is a medium-range Force attack. Think of it as a powerful Force push that causes damage as it impacts your opponent and also when the opponent hits a wall or the ground. Because it pushes your opponent away, it is difficult to follow up with slashes after this attack.

The Whirlwind Strike is a move more like contemporary Jedi dueling and features several slashing spins that cause damage to the opponent and knocks them off their feet.

The Electric Toss is a grapple move that uses the Force to damage the opponent and throws them for additional damage. This attack does not use Force from the meter, so you can use it while your meter builds up or if you're saving Force for another special attack.

The Clearing Spin is basically a fast slash combo with a powerful spin attack at the end. Therefore, you can use it just like you would a normal combo. While the opponent may block the first two slashes, the Force-filled spin at the end usually connects for some damage and can be unexpected.

COMBAT CHARTS

Basic Controls

Name	Xbox	PS2
Saber throw	WHT	L2
Force push/grasp	R	R1
Target select	R	Right analog
Strafe	Hold L+→	Hold L1 + Left analog →
Force lightning	BL	R2
Force heal	Click L+R	Click left analog + right analog
Force speed	→,→	Left analog →, left analog →

Special Attacks

Name	Xbox	PS2
Force Lightning Explosion	Hold X	Hold ■
Whirlwind Strike	Hold Y	Hold ▲
Electric Toss	X+Y,Y	■+▲,▲
Clearing Spin	X,X,Y+X	■,■,▲+■

General Grievous

General Grievous is the only non-Jedi duelist available in the game. However, this droid is still capable of dueling using his two—or four—lightsabers. Because Grievous is not a Jedi, Force powers such as push, grasp, and heal are not available to him. Therefore, any health lost during a duel can't be replaced.

Grievous's Force Clear Out attack is a close-range, spinning attack that hits nearby opponents several times and knocks them back. This unblockable attack is a good starting move and will put your opponent on the defensive immediately.

General Grievous begins with only two lightsabers, but activate Four Arm mode to bring out two more arms, each with their own lightsaber for a total of four. This ability uses up Force from the meter, and when the meter is empty, the two extra arms return to their initial position.

While this is not an attack of its own, this ability does increase the damage done by every slash and combo Grievous can't

throw a lightsaber, but his Fire Blaster attack gives him a ranged attack as well. Quickly push the appropriate button to fire off quick shots with the blaster. Hold down the button to build up a charge for a more damaging shot. Each shot uses up Force from the meter.

The 3 Variation Charge-Up is a dash attack. Hold down the appropriate button and Grievous crouches down and builds up power. When you release, the droid runs at the opponent and engages in a kicking and throwing attack. However, this attack is linear, so a quick-thinking opponent will jump out of the way, since the charge-up crouch indicates that the attack is coming.

COMBAT CHARTS

Basic Controls

Name	Xbox	PS2
Target select	N/A	N/A
Strafe	Hold L+↔	Hold L1 + Left analog ⇨

Special Attacks

Name	Xbox	PS2
Force Clear	Hold Y	Hold ▲
Four Arm mode	WHT	L2
Fire Blaster (hold to charge)	R	R1
3 Variation Charge-Up	BLN	R2

Mace Windu

Mace Windu features all of the standard Jedi attacks and Force powers. In addition, many of his special attacks use the Force to increase the power and damage caused by his lightsaber slashes and thrusts. Unlike some of the other duelists, all of Mace's special attacks are close range. Therefore, keep Mace right next to your opponent, using basic combos and slashes until you are ready to unleash a special attack.

The Force Clear Out is a single-button attack that acts as a short-range dash attack. Mace rushes through his opponents, knocking them off their feet, leaving them open for a follow-up attack.

Another powerful single-button attack is the Force Charge. While this is more of a slashing short dash attack, its effects are similar to the Force Clear Out.

A Back Kick Flip is a special grapple attack that can do some serious damage to your opponent. If you don't grapple much, this is one attack that might change your mind.

The Launching Uppercut is a tough attack to perform. It is essentially a basic combo with a twist at the end. Practice this and when you have it down, you will be impressed at how well this attack works during a duel—it damages the enemy and acts as a throw at the end for further damage.

COMBAT CHARTS

Basic Controls

Name	Xbox	PS2
Saber throw	WHT	L2
Force push/grasp	R	R1
Target select	R	Right analog
Strafe	Hold L+→	Hold L1 + Left analog →
Force stun	L	R2
Force heal	Click L+R	Click left analog + right analog
Force speed	→,→	Left analog →, left analog →

Special Attacks

Name	Xbox	PS2
Force Clear Out	Hold X	Hold ■
Force Charge	Hold Y	Hold ▲
Back Kick Flip	X+Y,X	■+▲,■
Launching Uppercut	X,X,→+Y	■,■, left analog → + ▲

Serra Keto

Serra Keto has all of the Jedi powers one would expect of a light side Jedi. What makes her a bit different is that she wields two lightsabers, making her attacks wider and a bit more damaging. She also has some interesting special attacks that allow her to engage her opponent at close to medium range.

While Serra can throw a lightsaber just like any Jedi, her Dual Saber Toss is a special attack where she throws both lightsabers at her target, inflicting more damage than a single saber throw. Use this if you have Force in your meter and want to damage an enemy who is preparing to heal or who is preparing an attack against you.

The Force Spiral is a dashlike attack. Face your opponent at medium range, then use this attack to quickly close on them, causing some serious damage and knocking them down.

Serra also has a good grapple attack. Her Kick Flip Launch begins with a grapple, pulling her opponent back and then setting up for a two-foot kick that launches the opponent into the air. When playing as Serra, this is a must-use attack when you are at close range. It also doesn't require Force from your meter.

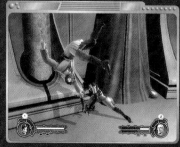

The Clearing Slam starts off as a fast slash combo, but ends with a grapple where Serra throws her opponent to the ground. Again, this attack does not require Force from the meter, so it can be followed with any Force attack.

COMBAT CHARTS

Basic Controls

Name	Xbox	PS2
Saber throw	WHT	L2
Force push/grasp	R	R1
Target select	A	Right analog
Strafe	Hold L+→	Hold L1 + Left analog ⇨
Force stun	BLK	R2
Force heal	Click L+R	Click left analog + right analog
Force speed	→,→	Left analog ⇨, left analog ⇨

Special Attacks

Name	Xbox	PS2
Dual Saber Toss	Hold X	Hold ■
Force Spiral	Hold Y	Hold ▲
Kick Flip Launch	X+Y,Y	■+▲,▲
Clearing Slam	X,X,Y+X	■,■,▲+■

Cin Drallig

Cin Drallig is a Jedi Master and one of the main trainers at the Jedi Temple. Therefore, he is an expert in the dueling arts and is very capable with basic combos and Force powers. His special attacks use the Force to accelerate his actions to the point where he appears as a blur[—o fast his opponents have no chance to react and block against him.

The 1000 Slashes is a close-range attack activated by a single press of a button. Using his incredible speed, Cin moves from side to side in a rapid motion, slashing away as he goes. This damages your opponent and can unnerve them since they are unable to react.

While standing apart from your opponent at medium range, use the Double Force Blast to launch two Force energy balls at your opponent. They knock down the opponent, allowing Cin to move in for some follow-up attacks.

The Clearing Slam is essentially a Force hit at a combo's end and is a way to add a bit more damage to a combo without having to use any Force power.

The Five Point Strike begins as a grapple but ends with five quick slashes against which your opponent can't block. This attack does not require Force power from the meter.

COMBAT CHARTS

Basic Controls

Name	Xbox	PS2
Saber throw	WHT	L2
Force push/grasp	R	R1
Target select	R	Right analog
Strafe	Hold L + →	Hold L1 + Left analog →
Force stun	LK	R2
Force heal	Click L + R	Click left analog + right analog
Force speed	→, →	Left analog →, left analog →

Special Attacks

Name	Xbox	PS2
1000 Slashes	Hold X	Hold ■
Double Force Blast	Hold Y	Hold ▲
Clearing Slam (at end of combo)	Y + X	▲ + ■
Five Point Strike	X + Y, X	■ + ▲, ■

Darth Vader

Darth Vader has learned some new tricks since his duel with Obi-Wan on Mustafar. Able to perform all of the combos and Force powers of a Dark Jedi, Vader is a formidable opponent. While not quite as fast as some of the other duelists, Vader's attacks are damaging and very effective.

Darth Vader's own signature grapple attack, the Force Choke holds the opponent suspended in midair while the health is drained from his or her body.

The Fury Slam is a powerful attack that damages a nearby opponent and throws them back, leaving them open for a follow-up combo attack.

The Clearing Spin begins as a fast slash combo, but ends with a Force-powered spin attack. It is important that you stay in close to your opponent when using this attack or the spin will miss.

The Backhand Lunge is a powerful attack. However, you must move directly toward your opponent or you may totally miss them, expending Force for no effect.

COMBAT CHARTS

Basic Controls

Name	Xbox	PS2
Saber throw	(WHT)	L2
Force push/grasp	(R)	R1
Target select	(A)	Right analog
Strafe	Hold (L)+→	Hold L1 + Left analog →
Force lightning	(BL)	R2
Force heal	Click (L)+(A)	Click left analog + right analog
Force speed	→,→	Left analog →, left analog →

Special Attacks

Name	Xbox	PS2
Force Choke	(X)+(Y)	■+▲
Fury Slam	Hold →+(Y)	Hold Left analog → + ▲
Clearing Spin	(X),(X),(Y)+(X)	■,■,▲+■
Backhand Lunge	Hold →+(B)	Hold Left analog → + ●

A. B. C.

Ben Kenobi

Ben Kenobi has some similar actions to his younger self when he went by the name Obi-Wan. However, over the years, he has developed some new and effective attacks that can be damaging against his opponents.

The Saber Bump is Ben's grapple attack. It consists of a kick followed by a blow to the opponent's head with the hilt of Ben's lightsaber.

The Force Shockwave is a Force-based attack that causes damage to your opponent and throws them across the room, causing more damage. This is a good way to break up an opponent's combo, and it gives you a chance to heal or prepare for another attack.

By adding a grapple button press following two fast slash attacks, Ben performs a Clearing Slam that pushes back his opponent a bit and opens them up for a follow-up attack—even if the opponent was successfully blocking the beginning slashes of the combo.

The Force Submission action converts Ben's health into Force, giving him a chance to conduct some Force-powered attacks, but at the cost of being very susceptible to losing the duel if his opponent can land a hit or two.

COMBAT CHARTS

Basic Controls

Name	Xbox	PS2
Saber throw	WHT	L2
Force push/grasp	R	R1
Target select	R	Right analog
Strafe	Hold L + →	Hold L1 + Left analog →
Force stun	BLK	R2
Force heal	Click L+R	Click left analog + right analog
Force speed	→, →	Left analog →, left analog →

Special Attacks

Name	Xbox	PS2
Saber Bump	X+Y	■+▲
Force Shockwave	Hold →+Y	Hold Left analog → + ▲
Clearing Slam	X,X,Y+X	■,■,▲+■
Force Submission	Hold L,B+X	Hold L1,●+■

Duel Arenas

After you choose two duelists, select an arena for the duel. There are 14 arenas from which to choose—each with their own unique characteristics. In order to be a successful duelist, you must know the arena and how to use it to your advantage.

Throne Room Main Chamber

This arena is actually the first area where you engage in a duel during the single-player story missions. In that mission, you could move around the entire area, but for the multiplayer duel, the Throne Room Main Chamber consists only of the area near the windows. This makes it a bit tighter with less room to move around. However, this small size also allows for throwing your opponent against a wall or edge of the arena and slashing away as they slowly drop to the floor. There is nothing for you to throw here, so the only damage inflicted on your enemy must be done by yourself.

Throne Room Upper Balcony

This area is long but narrow. The balcony wraps around in a semicircle with a couple bends at the ends. There is sufficient room to get away from your opponent if you need to heal or set up for a ranged or dash attack. In addition, there are several objects that you can throw. You can throw the cylindrical objects hanging on the walls, and you can throw your opponent into them for additional damage. A good tactic is to push your opponent into a corner. Because of this arena's narrowness, he or she will be boxed in, with little room to maneuver. A combination of a Force attack, such as push or stun, and slashing combos will help lead to the end of your trapped opponent.

Utapau Sinkhole Control Room

The control room is a bit bigger than the previous arenas. In addition, there are lots and lots of objects which can be thrown including the chairs. While you cannot throw the computer consoles, you can throw your opponent into them. Due to the size of this arena, you have plenty of room around which to maneuver. If your opponent tries a dash attack, jump to one side and avoid it. If necessary, there is also room to withdraw to heal or get away from an aggressive opponent's incessant attacks.

DUEL ARENAS

Utapau Sinkhole Landing Platform

The landing platform is another large arena. There are also several objects you can throw, including pylons and rocks. Because it is wide open throughout the middle, ranged and dash attacks work well here, though an opponent does have room to evade the attack if not executed quickly enough. When dueling here, keep moving and avoid getting backed up against the arena's edge.

Palpatine's Office Docking Bay

This large arena offers a lot of maneuver room and some narrow areas such as the balcony at the rear. There are also several lights, consoles, and other objects that you can throw. The key here is to keep moving so you are more difficult to target with thrown objects, ranged attacks, and linear dash attacks. Because of the space, this is also a great place for duelists who have grapple attacks that involve throwing or kicking.

Palpatine's Office

While Palpatine's Office is not small, the furniture and other objects make it seem confining. The couches on the side and the table at the rear break up the room. They can also offer a barrier that your opponent must either move around or jump over in order to reach you. There are several objects that you can throw using the Force, including chairs, small tables, and even the two large statues near the area's front. Because of the room's layout, it is easy to get backed into a corner—try doing this to your opponent. If your opponent tries to put a barrier between you and them, throw your lightsaber at them or Force throw them toward you to illustrate that no matter where your opponent may run, you can always attack.

Temple Training Room

The Temple Training Room is set up perfectly for duels. It offers a large open area in which to fight. This arena also features the largest number of objects that you can pick up and throw using the Force. In addition to the objects on stands around the center and the large chunks of broken statues, there are shelves on the right and left filled with small spheres that explode when they hit someone. If you are good at Force throws, you can actually defeat your opponents by just hitting them with objects found in the room. On the other hand, if you are having those spheres thrown at you, throw your opponent into the shelves and blow up all of the spheres at one time.

Temple Control Room

This is a challenging arena that a good Jedi can actually use against his or her opponent. In addition to the rocks, helmets, and other objects that you can throw, there is also an electrical arc at the arena's rear. Throw or push your opponent into the arc and they will receive some shocking damage. Don't accidentally move into the arc during the heat of the duel since the shock will damage you and also force you to drop your blocking action, opening you to attacks by your opponents.

Temple Outer Terrace

The Outer Terrace is a wide-open area. While there is a battle going on around you, it is just for show—even though some areas at the arena's edge take damage. While there is no place to hide, making ranged and dash attacks useful, there are several things you can throw. Move your right analog stick around to target chunks from the wall and pieces of the flooring. You will be surprised by what you can throw here. Even though this arena is wide-open, you can push your opponent into one of the corners to cut down on their maneuver room and limit their options. In fact, cornering an opponent and then launching a dash attack can be very effective here.

Mustafar Control Room

While the Control Room is rather large, the two holographic projection tables in the center really break it up. While there is nothing here to throw, you can throw your opponent into the consoles that surround the room. While in the center you have quite a bit of maneuver room, so use appropriate attacks. Use ranged attacks to hit your opponent if he or she moves around one of the tables to get away from you. A saber throw or Force attack can stun them enough for you to get around and start slashing. If you must get away to heal, there is plenty of space. Just throw your opponent to one side of the room, then run for the opposite side and get in some healing before the duel continues.

Mustafar Balcony

The Balcony is fairly small, forcing both duelists to get in close and go at it. There are some objects that you can throw here; however, be careful you don't hit yourself or get caught in the explosion. Because of the arena's size, there is little chance you can avoid your opponent's attacks. Therefore, unless you can quickly Force heal while your opponent is down or stunned, you are usually better off keeping up the attack and eliminating your opponent before he or she eliminates you.

DUEL ARENAS

Mustafar Control Arm

The Mustafar Control Arm is a challenging arena. It is straight, narrow, and long. Because of its length, it is easy to miss with a dash attack because you are farther away from your opponent than you realize. While it does get a bit wider at the arm's left end, where you can maneuver more side to side, the arena's center and right parts force opponents into a linear battle. With nothing to pick up and throw here, you must inflict all the damage yourself; you can throw your opponent against objects, but they are only at either end of the arena. This arena definitely favors the player who likes to get in and fight without having to worry about an opponent jumping out of the way.

Mustafar Lava Platform

If you thought some of the earlier arenas were small, just wait until you try the Mustafar Lava Platform. This arena is downright tiny. It is a good thing there is nothing to throw here because chances are you would just hit yourself. Due to the small size, duels here are often quick and consist of constant action. You can never get out of range of a saber throw to heal, so your best bet, unless you can stun your opponent with a powerful attack, is to keep fighting. If you don't know how to block or shunt, you are toast here since there is nowhere to run or jump to avoid your opponent. Grappling also works well since you are almost always in grapple range of your opponent.

Episode IV Death Star

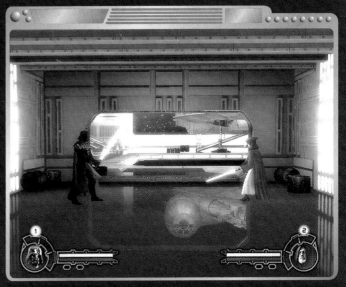

This is one of the coolest arenas in the game—not because it has a lot of neat features, but because it is from Star Wars Episode IV: A New Hope. This is where the world first saw a Jedi duel, and everyone loves a classic. Overall, the Death Star arena is fairly sparse. There are a few objects in the corners that you can throw, but other than that, it is wide-open. If you like to trap your opponent to limit his or her mobility, push them back into one of the alcoves on either the right or left side and slash away. This arena is also good for jumping and dash attacks since you have some space to move, but you don't have much room to avoid such an attack.

Challenge Mission 1: Cruiser Cargo Hold

As you progress through the single-player missions, you unlock four challenge missions. These cooperative missions allow you to play along with another person, working together to defeat your enemies. To complete these missions successfully, support your partner and communicate often. Read on for more strategies.

Briefing

Characters: Anakin and Obi-Wan

Location: Separatist Cruiser

The Separatist cruiser's cargo hold is crawling with droids. Before they can rescue the kidnapped chancellor, Obi-Wan and Anakin must combine their Jedi skills to clear the room.

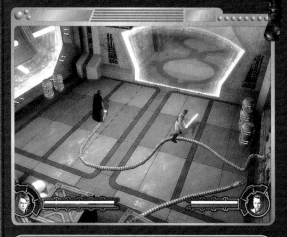

Objective
• Destroy Separatist droids

Walkthrough

This mission pits you and a friend, or a computer-controlled ally, against waves of droids that attack you. You begin in an enclosed area. Battle droids approach through the crates at the screen's bottom and through the force field at the top.

> **TIP**
>
> In the Challenge missions, it is vital that you communicate with your fellow Jedi. Let him or her know your status and if you need help. It is a good idea to divide up and cover separate parts of the area, but for tough opponents, consider coming together and ganging up, with one Jedi attacking the front, forcing the opponent to block while the second Jedi slashes away at the unprotected back or side.

A good strategy is to split up the area, with one Jedi covering the right side while the other covers the left. Since most of the battle droids enter through the crates, hang out around there, using Force powers such as push and throw to deal with those coming through the force field.

Eventually you must deal with super battle droids and grapple droids. Focus on the super battle droids first since their blasters can cause you a lot of damage.

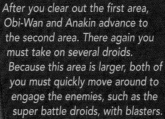

TIP

There are no bacta tanks on this level. Therefore, if you take damage, you must Force heal yourself. Keep track of your own health and that of your fellow Jedi. If he or she gets low, offer to cover them while they heal up.

Use teamwork on the grapple droids. A quick Force push can stun one of these droids while your fellow Jedi starts slicing and dicing the menacing hulk of a droid.

After you clear out the first area, Obi-Wan and Anakin advance to the second area. There again you must take on several droids. Because this area is larger, both of you must quickly move around to engage the enemies, such as the super battle droids, with blasters.

After a bit, destroyer droids start rolling in. Quickly stun them with your Force powers, then move in for the kill. Destroyers become your priority target as soon as they arrive. Whichever Jedi has more Force on the meter should be tasked with stunning these droids.

Continue fighting until all enemies have been defeated to complete this first challenge mission.

Challenge Mission 2: Cruiser Corridors

Briefing

Characters: Anakin and Obi-Wan

Location: Separatist Cruiser

The ever-dependable astromech droid R2-D2 comes under fire from the Separatist forces, and only his Jedi protectors Obi-Wan Kenobi and Anakin Skywalker can lead him to safety.

NEW OBJECTIVE: DEFEAT SEPARATIST FORCES

Objective
• Defeat Separatist forces

Walkthrough

Once again, Anakin and Obi-Wan are fighting off droids. You begin in another small area and must engage droids that enter through doorways on the right and left. Split up with one Jedi covering each doorway.

Use the same teamwork tactics you used in the previous challenge mission and you will have little trouble taking out the battle droids and super battle droids that come at you.

NOTE

The powers and attacks of most Jedi in the challenge missions are set. You get the same special attacks for these characters that they get in the multiplayer duels.

With the first area clear, R2-D2 lowers the force field, allowing you to advance to the next area. This is a bit tougher because you must now deal with destroyer droids as well as the other two types (battle and super droids). This area is also quite small, so it can get confusing. Just remember to stun the destroyers to make them drop their shields, then move in for the kill.

Use Force throw to pull super battle droids on the other side of the force field toward the field, where they will be damaged or even destroyed. When it gets crowded, throw droids at each other so you can damage two droids instead of one.

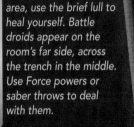

As you enter the third area, use the brief lull to heal yourself. Battle droids appear on the room's far side, across the trench in the middle. Use Force powers or saber throws to deal with them.

Super battle droids soon crawl up out of the trench. Focus on these more powerful droids, slashing away at them before they get a chance to fire at you.

When R2-D2 provides a bridge across the trench, move to the room's other side. There are force fields on the right and left through which battle droids will come at you.

One Jedi should cover the force field on the left while the other covers the right. By destroying the battle droids when they come through the force field, or even before, you can prevent being shot at.

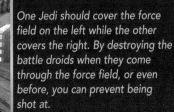

The final area is a medium-sized room with several explosive containers. Stay away from them as much as possible so you are not caught in the blast if a stray blaster shot or lightsaber slash hits one. Take out the battle droids that come at you.

New Objective

• Defeat Grievous' bodyguards

The final enemies you must deal with are Grievous' bodyguards. These are tough droids to destroy. However, with two Jedi, the task is much easier when you use the Force.

TIP

If there are still explosive containers around, throw them at Grievous' bodyguards for a hard-hitting and damaging blow.

If possible, gang up on a single bodyguard and slash away. While bodyguards are pretty good at blocking a single attacker, they don't stand a chance against two determined Jedi. After you eliminate all of the bodyguards, the mission is complete.

STAR WARS
EPISODE III
REVENGE OF THE SITH

Challenge Mission 3: Control Sphere Survival

Briefing

Characters: Obi-Wan and Anakin

Location: Utapau

Obi-Wan and Anakin must fight through a seemingly endless wave of droid forces on their way to the Separatists' control center.

Objective
- **Defeat Separatist attackers**

Walkthrough

This challenge mission takes place all in one area. Don't worry, the enemy comes to you. The mission begins fairly easy and becomes more difficult as you progress. The first enemies you face are buzz droids. Just slash away to destroy them.

TIP

Because of this area's size and the many entrances that the droids will use, it is hard to divide up this area between the two Jedi. So, work together and inform your partner of new threats as they arrive or if you need some assistance.

Since this area is rather large, super battle droids can be a problem. They can enter through doorways on the right and left sides as well as through two doorways at the area's back. Jump as you move toward them and take them out as quickly as possible to minimize the damage they can do with their blasters.

Destroyer droids and grapple droids attack you at the same time. Stun the destroyers first, eliminate them, then go after the grapple droids; be careful not to get caught in their metallic embrace.

With all of the damage you will take, keep some Force on the meter so you can heal yourself as needed. The pause between waves is ideal for this.

The next wave consists of air battle droids. These droids are equipped with an arm shield that can block your lightsaber, so either take them out while they are in the air or Force stun or push them to get in a slash.

The final part of the mission is the toughest. You must take on five turrets at once. Three rise out of the floor and two come out of the walls at the back. You will have trouble Force deflecting all of them, so go on the attack. Use powerful combos to take out the turrets on the floor, and use saber throws for the turrets on the wall. Stick together with your fellow Jedi and clear out one section of turrets at a time, beginning on one side and working your way across so you don't have turrets firing at you from all directions. After you destroy the turrets, you have won this challenge mission.

Challenge Mission 4: The Jedi Strike Back

Briefing

Characters: Serra Keto and Cin Drallig

Location: Coruscant

Jedi Master Cin Drallig and his apprentice Serra Keto engage the invading clone forces in the Jedi Temple, driving back the troopers' aggression with Jedi strength and skill.

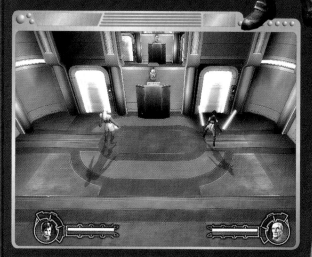

Objective
• Defeat Separatist forces

Walkthrough

For this challenge mission, these two Jedi must progress through a series of areas. In each area, when no enemies remain, a console is revealed. Access this console to lower the force fields to the next area.

The first area is just a console. In the second area, you face only clone troopers. They are not very tough, and the two Jedi have no trouble defeating them.

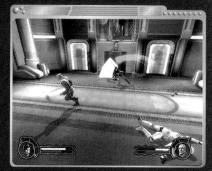

TIP

Since you determine when you enter the next level (by accessing the consoles), take time to heal back to maximum and let your Force meter build up as well. Therefore, when you start the next area, you are fresh and ready to fight.

The third area adds clone heavy gunners to the mix. These clones hide in the doorways where they are difficult to see, depending on the viewing angle. Usually you don't know they are there until you see their weapon firing. To avoid being hit, stay out of the strip down the area's middle; use Force throws to pull these clones out into the middle where you can properly engage them.

The fourth area features two turrets—one over each doorway at the area's back. Take them out quickly before clones start arriving. Rather than Force deflecting the turrets' fire (which takes too long), throw your lightsaber at them or jump up and slash at them. Then deal with the clone troopers that come after you.

The fifth area is very similar to the last one. Again you face two turrets at the beginning. However, this time, there are objects in the room. Use the Force to throw these at the turrets to destroy them.

TIP

From the fourth area, you can actually destroy the turrets in the fifth area. Use the Force to pick up the objects and then throw them at the turrets. Then when you enter this next area, there are no turrets to deal with.

In addition to clone troopers, you must now deal with clone blaze troopers. Stay in close to them and keep slashing so they can't grapple or use their flamethrowers on you.

After the previous areas, the sixth area is quite easy. You only face clone troopers here. There is also a large container in the room's center. If it takes some damage, it explodes, causing damage to anyone nearby.

The seventh area can be tough. In addition to the clone troopers on the ground, clone heavy gunners appear on the upper alcoves on the right and left sides. These enemies fire down on you and are difficult to engage. To neutralize these heavy gunners, target them with the Force, then pull them down to the ground where you can properly slash them.

The final area of this challenge mission pits you against clone troopers and clone walkers. These large enemies shoot at you, and they can step on you.

As a Jedi Master, Cin Drallig can stun more than one enemy at a time. Use him to stun the troopers controlling the walkers, then move in and start slashing at their legs.

Don't worry about the clone troopers firing at you from the back of the area. The walkers are your main targets; deal with them first. After you eliminate the first two walkers, two more arrive to attack.

As you destroy the computer terminal at the back of the area, you reveal a saber crystal secret. Continue attacking until you eliminate all clones to complete this final challenge mission.

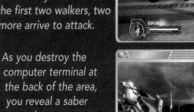

SECRET FOUND

Interview with Anthony Doe

Lead Combat Designer/Scripter, The Collective

Anthony Doe, right, helping Nick Gillard, left, demonstrate moves.

Q: What was it like having Hayden Christensen and Nick Gillard there to assist in your development of the game? Just how much did their input affect the final result?

Anthony Doe: It was one of those true highlights in making the game. A great experience. From the beginning, Nick showed us the basics of Jedi combat: the stances, attacks, defenses, and philosophies. It was a kind of modern-day Jedi training. The best part was that it was really all geared toward *us*, the game developers, to create the most authentic Jedi action experience yet seen in a video game. It's the reason why Nick brought in his good friend, Hayden Christensen, to work with us.

Hayden had trained a considerable time with Nick for **Episode III.** It *definitely* showed. He impressed us all by showing some serious talent with the practice saber (much more so than in the previous films). Together they showed us not only some of the brilliant **Episode III** fight choreography, but also acted out custom content for the game! All of this will show in the final product. The influence of Nick and Hayden will be seen in every swing of the player's lightsaber. You can't help but feel it when you play the game.

Nick says you guys had some pretty elaborate lightsaber fights of your own.

There was a video we put together that he was impressed by. That's the thing—as combat designers at The Collective, we act out fights. It's part of our daily routine—our bread and butter. A lot of us are martial artists, so it comes naturally. In researching for **Episode III**, we pored over all the movies, looked at previous *Star Wars* games, and even some of the early **Episode III** fight choreography. We took that to heart, acted out the moves and captured it on video. It's really for our own sake to make better fighting characters for the game. Although, I will admit, it's pretty fun to do also.

Any funny stories from Nick and Hayden's clinic that you can share?

One of the days, Nick was showing us some advanced lightsaber stuff. He just finished demonstrating a really wicked saber combo, stepping through in a blur of practice-saber trails, spinning in 360s and powerful imaginary killing blows. "And now," he said, "for something really dangerous."

"What could that be?" we all imagined. "An even deadlier saber technique?"

He paused, stepped forward, and then...broke out into a back spin. It was Jedi breakdancing!

The next thing you know, our director is doing the moonwalk...which was, umm...strange. All in all, it was pretty hilarious. I guess you had to be there.

What's the hardest part about making the combat system for the Episode III video game?

With Nick directing us, it was a piece of cake! Really, it was great to have worked with him and Hayden. The hardest part was taking that all in, digesting the *many* dozens of moves they showed, and making it live and breathe in the game. So you will see over a hundred unique player character abilities, from swinging the saber through seemingly countless combos, to delivering some deadly Force powers, to engaging the **Episode III** characters themselves in saber-lock battles. You'll see this minted in the different styles of Anakin, Obi-Wan, Dooku, Mace and all the other Jedi you'll be able to play as.

Getting all that to work with that "*Star Wars* feeling" we all know and love was the challenge. We faced that as our everyday goal for over a year. It has always been our goal to create "the ultimate Jedi action experience." Will we deliver on this? Well, let's just say I'm very proud of what will hit the shelves in May.

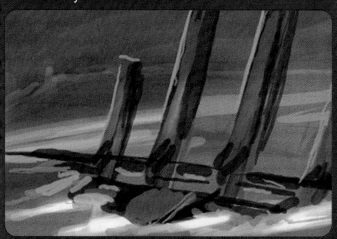

How does the Force come into play in the game?

The Force is your special sauce in combat—your personal can of whoop-ass. Whether you are good or evil, you'll be able to use the Force in fun and destructive ways. Imagine whimsically knocking over a squad of droids with just a hand gesture. Or grabbing that explosive canister from afar, and hurling it at Count Dooku! Feeling a little injured? You can Force heal yourself, too. Then again, if you just want to destroy more efficiently, the Force is there for you...giving you the ability to saber throw, cast lightning to fry your foes, or mind trick them into fighting on your side!

The Force is also part of the player's development as a character in the game. Whether playing as Anakin or Obi-Wan, the player will constantly gain experience and upgrade his library of Force powers. In addition, the player will unlock some really destructive special abilities and signature moves which also use Force power. The amount you have is measured in a Force power bar that constantly regenerates over time.

How different are the fighting styles of Anakin and Obi-Wan?

They are as different as their personalities. Anakin is the raw talent, unrefined, passionate and strong. He's got that cocky assuredness of someone who knows he's the best. You see this in Anakin's style: flashy yet efficient, direct and powerful, arrogant, unrestrained. He has a certain brooding demeanor. As Anakin turns to the dark side, his style will also become increasingly dark, and this will be seen in the "fury" moves that the player unlocks throughout the game.

By contrast, Obi-Wan is calm, focused, and controlled; he's the epitome of the classically trained Jedi Master. There's a certain gracefulness and constant flow to his moves. Whereas Anakin is more direct and "to the point," Obi-Wan swings with sweeping, controlled arcs. He "glides," as Nick described. In contrast to Anakin's power "fury" moves, Obi-Wan's unlockables we call his "focus" powers, which are all about speed and precision.

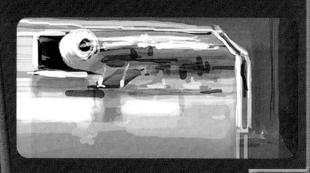

Interview with Nick Gillard

Stunt Coordinator

The following interview was conducted at ILM on January 14, 2004.

Nick Gillard on the computer.

Q: What are you doing here at ILM?

Nick Gillard: I'm over here at Lucasfilm working on the game for **Episode III**—hopefully working out the moves and the fights to get it as real as we can to the movie.

What have you been doing so far?

This week we've been working on breaking down the Jedi moves. Trying to work with the system—a written system that only a few of us know. Only the actors and the stunt guys do it, so I've been trying to teach the animators of the game and show the specific moves—show them how wrists move, how feet move—so we can get it as close as possible to the movie.

Have you been involved in a video game project before?

I've never been involved in a video game project. It's very new to me. In fact, I've only played three games, and it was, you know, knocking around with Hayden, who plays a lot. I caught up with him quick, and I'm now determined to win this game, because I'll know more about it than he will.

What are your thoughts on what you've seen of the game?

I've only seen the renderings of characters, but they look amazing. The set's exactly what we have in the film.

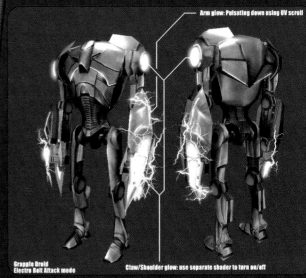

Grapple Droid
Electro Bolt Attack mode

Arm glow: Pulsating down using UV scroll

Claw/Shoulder glow: use separate shader to turn on/off

What's your approach to working on a film project? How is it different to work on the game?

On a movie, obviously I have a script. I know the story of the movie. I know how the characters are feeling, why they're fighting, where they've got to go. I think it's going to be pretty much the same on this game. The sets are all the same. The characters are the same. I'm going to take the same approach—I'm just going to get it much more detailed because it's much tighter than it is on the movie, and there's so much more time with the game.

Are there any moves that didn't make the film but did make the game?

The glory of doing the game is that there are lots of moves that don't work on the movie. They might be too complicated, or they might be too fierce, and get rejected for the film—we can now put those into the game.

Would you say you have more freedom to draw up fights in the video game world?

Yeah, I think that the game is going to give a whole lot of freedom because you can be so much more extreme. When we do the movie, it has to be believable. But I think with a game it should be more unbelievable.

INTERVIEWS

Is there something particular you're looking forward to seeing in the game?

Yes. I'm in the game. I'm really excited to see how I look in the game. My character in the game is larger than he is in the film—it's only a hologram in the film. And I'm going to try my damnedest to make him a character that nobody can actually beat, and you have to lure him onto something to kill him. I think he could certainly take out Anakin without any trouble at all (*laughs*).

Can you tell us more about the character in the movie?

I only did it providing my name could be my own name. So I have my own name backward. Which is Cin Drallig. I play an instructor, and I get killed by Anakin (*laughs*). Obviously in real life, I'd cream him.

Working with the video game team, have there been any pleasant surprises?

Yeah, there's been a huge difference between working with the video game team as opposed to Lucasfilm. It's that they're all like 17 years old (*laughs*)! You can't impress them as much. So in a way it's been harder.

What was most important to teach the animators? What did you want to show them to make sure they create authentic fighting sequences?

Having played a few games myself, you're playing it thinking, "God, I wish I could do this in the game!" Or, "I wish this button did that." Because we're working on this game, we're in the position to do that. And also, in the games I've played, the character movement seems to be incorrect, and I know that the people here were keen on how they could fix that. So we're working particularly on the footwork—how exactly they

move. How their wrists move when they turn, that they turn the right way, that the blocks and grapples are correct. We spent a lot of time showing how Count Dooku walked, how Anakin walks now as opposed to how he walked in **Episode II**—which is different—and why Obi is so bouncy and jolly.

Tell us about your hands-on demonstration session for the team.

When I came, I brought three lightsabers out with me—the ones that we use on the movies, which the guys on the game got pretty excited about. I think they've been using, like, rolled-up bits of cardboard. Although, there's a couple of the animators who made their own lightsaber fights, which were just amazing. I mean, I watched these guys and thought, "You know, I could use these guys in the film."

Hayden Christensen, left, sparring with Nick Gillard, right.

Which lightsabers did you bring?

I brought Anakin's, Obi's, and mine. And they're all actually like the characters. They're all different lights, different weights, different lengths. I think it was good for the guys to see that and how it's not just a generic lightsaber. They all have their own weight. Obi's is always much thicker than everyone else's. Anakin's is longer.

What else did you like about doing a video game?

One of the things I found really exciting about the game is that it's easy on a film—you know, you get a script and you're going to go in a room where there's five guys in there, and you have to kill them. But you know how to kill those guys—it's scripted. With the game, there are all these strange little characters. A guy might just come in sweeping at your ankles. As soon as you stop him, you might get a chance to kick him, but he'll swing around at you from the other side. If someone else comes into the room, you've got to deal with another guy. You might have only kicked him once—he's still alive—so you're always looking over your shoulder for the Sweeper Guy because you know he's coming to cut your ankles off, and now you're dealing with Lunging Guy. It's way different from the movie and a great challenge. I've really enjoyed working on the game.

How do you look at the swordfights you design?

When I'm doing swordfights on movies, I pretty much treat it totally as a dance. The footwork is as important as the swordwork, so everything has to stay in synch. It's more like choreography than fight arranging.

Do you think about the characters involved when choreographing a fight scene?

When we started on *Phantom Menace*, I set out certain styles and, particularly, faults for characters. Once you know the line of them, you know why they're going to do something. You know why they're going to behave a certain way, what's going to make them angry or not angry. It's very easy to just knock through a fight. If you know the script and you know why they're there—where they're going, why they're going there—it makes the whole thing much easier.

Do you take into account the use of sound and special effects when you're looking to do a scene or sequence?

I have tapes that I get from Ben Burtt of lightsaber noises. The sound effects and the lighting effects can help you a great deal—you know what's going on. You know there are explosions or flashes of light. It makes it a whole lot easier.

How was it to work with Ewan McGregor and Hayden Christensen? Especially on such a long and arduous fight?

The fight with Anakin and Obi-Wan at the end is an incredibly long fight—I think it'll be the longest fight in cinema history. It was fantastic to work on. I had Hayden for maybe seven weeks of rehearsal. I tried to keep Hayden and Ewan apart for a long time. I would fight them against doubles, and I kept it right until the very end before they went against each other. And even then I think the two of them weren't too keen on that—you know, they wanted to almost save it for when we were shooting. Because it's so emotional.

How would you say Obi-Wan evolves as a swordsman from Episode I to Episode III?

Obi-Wan has gone up one level from **Episode I** to **Episode III**, but it's a huge jump from one level to another. It's not just about a style of fighting—it's mental as well. Anakin has gone up probably four levels from **Episode II** to **Episode III**. So he's gone beyond Obi-Wan, but he hasn't gone beyond him mentally.

How has Anakin's style changed?

Anakin's style has changed completely between **Episode II** and **Episode III**. He now no longer cares. He knows he's unbeatable. He's far more dangerous than anybody in the universe.

If you could arrange a fight scene between any two *Star Wars* characters, who would they be?

The fight I'd really like to see would be Boba Fett versus Anakin.

What's been your favorite fight sequence from Episodes I through III?

Without question, it's Obi-Wan versus Anakin in **Episode III.** One was the master, one was the pupil. One has replaced the other one, technically. Obi knows that Anakin is better than him, but because he taught him, he

knows emotionally how he's going to behave. I took it on as like a fight between a husband and wife. It sounds silly, but Obi doesn't want to kill him. Obi has got to try and withstand this onslaught—this huge onslaught that's going to cover like a mile and be 10 minutes long, which is an enormous amount of time for a fight. So I took it as Obi trying to take this onslaught continuously and hoping that Anakin was going to eventually, you know, get over it and calm down. That doesn't happen.

How do you choreograph things taking into account, say, Hayden's height advantage?

Height doesn't matter. It doesn't matter at all. I just work on what they have. Their faults, mostly. So I've always had a fault for both of them.

What's Anakin's particular fault?

Anakin has the least of them all, but his would be being on a slope.

How about Obi-Wan?

Obi's is his aggression. If he has a downfall, that's it.

What was the most difficult fight sequence in any *Star Wars* movie?

The first one, because it had been so long since the last movie—I may have been a bit flippant. I liked the fight with Obi-Wan and Darth Maul, but some seven years on, it's evolved so much. I've taken it so much more seriously. I understand it much better, so once I got to Obi-Wan versus Anakin, I really let it rip. But also keep it so true. On *The Phantom Menace*, it's the first time we've seen them fight that well. But by this last one, I think we had it in the bag—everybody knew how they should be. Everybody knew how it should look. There's so much pressure as well, because millions of fans also know how it should look, and you've got to try to stay true for them too.

When you first receive the script, how do you choreograph what you see on the page to what we finally see on the screen?

Usually in the script there's nothing at all. It just says, you know, "vicious fight," and so I just ask George how long he wants it. And then get the drawings of the sets and stuff, and go from there.

Is it hard to come up with something that's new and fresh?

Not for me because this has such a history. You know you can just go with it—you can take it to another level every time.

Do you draw inspiration for your choreography from things other than other fight scenes?

The only thing I draw them from would be real stuff, like I watch a lot of real footage of things. And if I see something I can borrow. I'd never take it from another film. I'd always hope they'd take it from us.

What are you most excited to see in the final cut of Episode III?

I'm just excited about the whole film. I really am just like everybody else—I just can't wait to see it!

How did you become interested in swordplay?

I was in the circus when I was a child, and I went from that into medieval jousting. I was like 16 when I started there. I learned all medieval weapons, and I sort of became interested in it, and so throughout my career, I've just picked up more and more reference.

Have you ever been mugged?

I was once in New York, which was a dreadful mistake. And once in Brighton, which was two of them making a dreadful mistake.

Interview with Justin Lambros, Associate Producer

What are your plans in the game for the evolution of Anakin Skywalker from Jedi hero to Sith villain?

The evolution of Anakin as a character in the game is going to be one of the most dynamic and exciting parts of it. You'll start working side-by-side with Obi-Wan Kenobi as you have been for years in the Clone Wars, and you'll be very similar. You'll fight together as a team, you'll use your lightsaber similarly, and you'll kind of be the standard Jedi heroic general that fought in the Clone Wars. But as it progresses and Anakin gives in to the dark side, then he's able to tap into a whole other side of the Force, and he's able to use powers that are much more dynamic and powerful and sinister and deadly. And so, as he evolves in the game, he ends up being much different than Obi-Wan. Obi-Wan stays true to the light side of the Force, and Anakin then becomes the maelstrom of power that we see that is feared throughout the galaxy.

What are your top priorities regarding the production of the game?

My top priority is to make sure that we stay on top of the film's development, every last little detail, every scene that changes, every editing sequence. Every time there's a change in the digital mattes in the background or the droids or anything that's changed, I want to make sure that we're on top of that because we're essentially making the game as ILM is making the film, so two different digital versions of these sequences are being created at the same time. And my job is to make sure that they match and they're accurate and we've got all the details correct because we want the game and the film to work together and mesh perfectly as one larger entity, not two separate products based on one story.

The game comes out two weeks before the movie. Would you recommend playing the game first or playing the game after you see the film?

I would recommend doing both, actually. The game does a great job telling the film's central conflict, but it's more visceral and very exciting to live it interactively. But we were very careful not to spoil key moments of the film. In fact, there's so much emotion and character development in **Episode III** that we'd never be able to cover that in a single game. And it's important to note that we're not just

re-creating the movie scene-for-scene in 3D. It's important that the game serves its medium, not just retells the film. So, we expand on the film in several key areas, and I think playing through the story mode of our game is a great taste of that emotional core which will leave you wanting more and, hopefully, heighten your anticipation for seeing the film. But after you get back from the theater, I think it'd be worth playing through the story mode again, this time with all the plot details fully revealed to you. So, you'll be able to see and feel more completely the path of Obi-Wan and Anakin in the game, making the action even more intense. You'll also understand how the events you're controlling in the game affect the rest of the galaxy.

So how closely will the game follow the movie, then?

Our game follows the plot of the film very closely, but it really focuses on—and in many cases expands—the central characters, Obi-Wan Kenobi and Anakin Skywalker, and their developing conflict. So we really concentrated on bringing their key action moments to life in the game. Our game runs the full spectrum from re-creating action sequences blow for blow and room for room, to delivering the full impact of sequences that are just introduced, or hinted at, by the film. In fact, we've actually included levels based on scenes that were written and shot for the film, but won't make the final cut. Our integration with George Lucas from early on really allowed us to expand on the film in ways that stay true to his original vision.

www.lucasarts.com/eps

INTERVIEWS

Tell us more about what's in the game but not the film.

What we wanted to do was expand upon ideas and scenes that were maybe cut short or just, you know, through the editing process don't appear very long in the film. We're able to then expand and fully realize different environments and attacks and events that may just be a minute or two in the film sequence, but then we'll get to show Anakin and Obi-Wan in their fullest, their most powerful, and give players then a chance to relive all those big exciting action sequences even larger and bigger than what is seen in the film.

So is there any particular scene you think is really cool?

The sequences at the end of the game once Anakin has fully realized his dark side power—that's when the player's going to have the widest array of movements and the most dynamic combo attacks and Force powers. Those will really be some of the most spectacular lightsaber combat we've ever seen in a

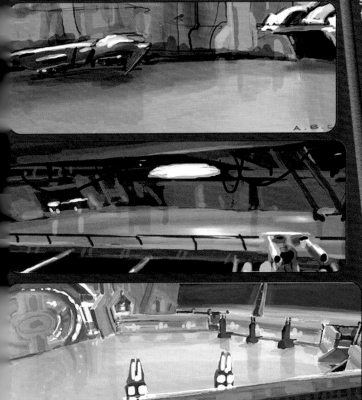

game, and that's what I'm really excited to see. Even expanding upon what we see in the film as we see him turn dark and sinister, we're going to take that and we're going to really run with it. And really make you understand why Darth Vader is this icon, this villain, this man who has helped control the galaxy.

And dueling against a friend is pretty cool, too, isn't it?

Yeah, one of the greatest aspects of this game is its fluid and deep combat system. What makes that combat system even more fun is using your mastery of it to school your buddies in the ways of the Jedi. As you fight your way through the plethora of intense lightsaber duels in the game, you will unlock enemies whom you've defeated in a two-player versus duel mode. So once you finish the game, you'll have a bunch of cool Jedi and Sith from **Episode III** to battle with against your friends. In fact, there may be a surprise or two waiting for you in that mode, as well. It's a fun and addictive addition to the single-player story mode, and since the control scheme for duels and adventure levels are the same, you'll be practicing to beat your friends as you live the story of **Episode III**.

Of course, the biggest duel in the game is the climactic fight between Obi-Wan and Anakin. Will it be as epic as the one in the film?

The lightsaber duel between Obi-Wan and Anakin in the movie is going to be one of the most extreme action sequences ever filmed. It's the greatest Jedi lightsaber duel ever, and we hope to take that and fulfill that dynamic, kinetic feeling of that film but then also a lot of the players who live it and expand upon it. And there'll be new areas, and new movements, new actions to really fulfill and play off all the energy and the power that's going between these two best friends turned bitter enemies. And so once we can really play off what we see in the film, we can go a whole other level of player involvement in that sequence. So it won't just be watching it up on a screen, it'll be reacting to Obi-Wan or Anakin's fighting and feeling their attack and feeling the ebb and flow of the battle. That's what I'm really excited about. We'll hopefully not only match the intensity, but then bring it up another level through interactivity.

How does combat differ as you progress through the game?

There's a wide variety of combat that you see in the film, and we want to represent that and make it even more diverse in the game. So when you're fighting the battle droids, the Jedi are able to cut through them, as they're not very strong. And then when you fight the clones—and the clones are much more organized, more tactical, with heavier firepower—they're able to think and react to your attacks and your movements, they'll be a much more difficult and more strategic opponent to battle. And then when you're fighting Jedi, that's a whole other level. They have powers, skills, and things that they're able to do, as well as battling against a lightsaber, which is the most powerful weapon in the galaxy. So we're going to see a wide variety of combat, and each will have its own niche and its own strategic element that you'll have to, as a player, know, learn, and repeat to be able to get through from one level to the next.

Episode III connects the dots between the prequel and classic films. Which classic connection are you most looking forward to?

When Darth Vader and Obi-Wan meet on the Death Star for their famous duel in the first *Star Wars* film, Darth Vader's, you know, famous line is, "The circle is now complete." Well, we're now going to be able to see, and actually live, the completing of that circle. The events that led up to this fateful duel and all of the emotion and baggage that comes with that, we're going to actually be able to not only show that onscreen but live that. We'll get the player to be able to see how Darth Vader became what he is today, and how Obi-Wan played a major part in that. And so we want to really get the backstory to complete that circle and show that that sequence in the Death Star was what that was all about.

How is this game different from other *Star Wars* games you've worked on?

This game is different from any other *Star Wars* game that I've worked on before in the fact that it's working so closely with the filmmakers, and we wanted to create that level of authenticity that is directly from the film. The game and the movie are one cohesive unit. They're not a couple of separate things. We're not trying to just create a version of the *Star Wars* universe to live in—we're trying to tell intricate parts of the *Star Wars* film **Episode III** and let you live those different sequences. Let you really feel what's going on in Anakin and Obi-Wan's minds as they go through this galaxy-changing event.

Did you look to any past *Star Wars* games for inspiration?

Yes, definitely. **Jedi Knight II: Jedi Outcast** and **Jedi Academy** had some really terrific saber fighting, so we looked at that. Our game was going to be very different, but we wanted to pull some of the strongest aspects of how that game made you feel like a Jedi and work them into our game, and then dial them up a few notches. The development team played **Knights of the Old Republic**, **Jedi Power Battles**, **Clone Wars**, **Bounty Hunter**, and any other *Star Wars* game we could get our hands on to try and identify the best *Star Wars* moments and ideas from those games.

What sets this game apart in terms of how it's being made?

What sets this game apart from any other *Star Wars* game that we've made has been how closely we've been working with ILM and Lucasfilm and Skywalker Sound, and being able to integrate all of the assets and everything that they're working on in production with the film. We've been able to get early versions of 3D models and characters and animations and sounds and edits of sequences, so we're able to use those things so as we construct our game and elaborate on the film and add to the sequences. We're able to use the authentic movie assets. And what's really going to shine through is we're going to have the most authentic, most realistic *Star Wars* experience that we're able to create and deliver.

INTERVIEWS

What makes Episode III stand out from other movie-based video games?

Several things, but first and foremost is the incredible level of involvement from everyone at all of the Lucasfilm companies, from members of the film's cast and crew, the concept artists at JAK, the digital wizards at ILM, the audiophiles from Sky Sound, and our biggest champions, our partners at Lucas Licensing. Starting at the very beginning, we got to meet with George Lucas to get his synopsis of the story before he even finished writing the first draft of the script, and his involvement continued through the concept art phase, through principal photography and into post-production.

Also, **Episode III** Producer Rick McCallum promised us "whatever we needed," and working with ILM and Lucas Licensing, he totally delivered. From getting the latest in-process digital assets to getting to see the practical models they build first-hand, to playing early versions of our game with Visual Effects Supervisor John Knoll, we got unprecedented access and support from ILM, without slowing down their incredible production rate.

Of course, Stunt Coordinator Nick Gillard schooled our development team on lightsaber combat and let us work with his star student, Hayden Christensen. And Skywalker Sound is handling all of the sound work to the large collection of in-game cutscenes, and delivering movie assets for all of the film footage sequences in the game. It's this kind of involvement and support

that has let our game developers make a fully authentic and exciting **Episode III** game that expands on the movie based upon information and ideas by the film's creators and contributors themselves.

What is the collaboration process like between LucasArts and ILM?

We're actually working very closely with ILM. They're the creators of all the digital assets for the film, so we get a chance to sit in on dailies, see the different scenes that they're working on, the different models that are coming to completion. And then we're also able to use the 3D models and the other images that they create, see the scenes as they're working on them so we can match the stuff that we're going to do in the game. And then also elaborate on it so we know where the game flows, how the characters move, that sort of thing. So we get a tremendous amount of insight and answers from the ILM team and their visual effects team there.

And with Lucasfilm?

We were able to see the art department's work—the early concept work they did. We've been able to shape our characters and know what we're going to be putting into the game just as they're doing that for the film. And also we've been able to have editorial visits with Lucasfilm, and that's been extremely important. We've been able to see the film change and evolve how sequences play out, and we're able to match that then in the game.

Experience and Skill

Earning Experience Points

The amount of experience points you earn for killing or destroying an enemy is dependent on your skill meter rating when the enemy is eliminated. The higher your skill meter rating, the greater the experience points earned. The following table lists the number of experience points earned for killing different enemies at the various skill meter ratings.

EXPERIENCE POINTS PER KILL

Enemy	Fair (1.0x)	Good (1.5x)	Impressive (2.0x)	Masterful (3.0x)
Battledroid	200	300	400	600
Battledroid Captain	300	450	600	900
Battledroid Sniper	300	450	600	900
Super Battledroid	400	600	800	1,200
Destroyer Droid	500	750	1,000	1,500
Grapple Droid (blue)	600	900	1,200	1,800
Grapple Droid (red)	800	1,200	1,600	2,400
Buzz Droid	200	300	400	600
Buzz Droid Dispenser	400	600	800	1,200
Flying Battledroid	500	750	1,000	1,500
Grievous Bodyguard	1,250	1,875	2,500	3,750
Crab Droid	3,000	4,500	6,000	9,000
Padawan	400	600	800	1,200
Jedi Sniper	600	900	1,200	1,800
Jedi Knight	800	1,200	1,600	2,400
Jedi Brute	1,000	1,500	2,000	3,000
Clone Trooper	300	450	600	900
Clone Sniper	400	600	800	1,200
Clone Heavy Gunner	500	750	1,000	1,500
Clone Blaze Trooper	700	1,050	1,400	2,100
Clone AT-ST Walker	900	1,350	1,800	2,700
Clone Assassin	1,000	1,500	2,000	3,000
Neimoidian Guard	350	525	700	1,050
Neimoidian Scout	500	750	1,000	1,500
Neimoidian Brute	1,000	1,500	2,000	3,000
Count Dooku	20,000	30,000	40,000	60,000
General Grievous	20,000	30,000	40,000	60,000
Mace Windu	22,500	33,750	45,000	67,500
Serra	10,000	15,000	20,000	30,000
Cin Drallig	15,000	22,500	30,000	45,000
Anakin	25,000	37,500	50,000	75,000
Small Turret	750	N/A	N/A	N/A
Banking Clan Cruiser	5,000	N/A	N/A	N/A
Jedi Starfighter	1,000	N/A	N/A	N/A
Clone Truck Cannon	1,000	N/A	N/A	N/A
Clone Truck (Defeated)	2,000	N/A	N/A	N/A
Clone Gunship	7,500	N/A	N/A	N/A
Neimoidian Shuttle	7,500	N/A	N/A	N/A

Maximizing Your Upgrades

In order for both Anakin and Obi-Wan to get all of the possible upgrades during the story missions, you must achieve a target amount of experience points for each mission. Since some missions have more enemies, or more powerful enemies, this target can vary by mission. The following table lists experience point targets for each mission. The last mission, "Revenge of the Sith," where you fight the final duel as Anakin, doesn't earn you experience points. Instead, it is like a bonus mission. For each character, you must gain 400,000 experience points in order to completely upgrade.

STORY MISSION EXPERIENCE-POINT TARGETS

Mission	Player Character	Experience-Point Target
Mission 1: Rescue over Coruscant	Anakin	30,000
Mission 2: An Explosive Development	Obi-Wan	60,000
Mission 3: Peril in the Elevators	Anakin	45,000
Mission 4: Settling the Score	Anakin	40,000
Mission 5: It's Not Over Yet	Anakin	30,000
Mission 6: The General's Right Hand	Anakin	20,000
Mission 7: Investigating Utapau	Obi-Wan	60,000
Mission 8: The Cavalry Arrives	Obi-Wan	60,000
Mission 9: Showdown with Grievous	Obi-Wan	40,000
Mission 10: The Dark Side of the Force	Anakin	45,000
Mission 11: The Hunt Begins	Anakin	70,000
Mission 12: The Final Lesson	Anakin	50,000
Mission 13: Attack of the Clones	Obi-Wan	60,000
Mission 14: Assassination on Mustafar	Anakin	70,000
Mission 15: Aftermath in the Temple	Obi-Wan	70,000
Mission 16: A Friendship in Flames	Obi-Wan	50,000

The Skill Meter

The skill meter is the curved meter that wraps partially around the portrait of your character. The meter tops out at 1,000 skill points. At the beginning of a mission, your character's skill meter is at zero. You gain skill points by attacking enemy units. You lose skill points when you are attacked or you go a period of time without attacking. The following tables list the amount of skill points you earn or lose for various actions.

primagames.com

SKILL POINTS AWARDED FOR SUCCESSFULLY STRIKING AND DAMAGING AN ENEMY

Type of Attack	Skill Points Awarded
Light Attack Hit	10
Enhanced Light Attack Hit	15
Strong Attack Hit	20
Enhanced Strong Attack Hit	25
Critical Attack Hit	30
Enhanced Critical Attack Hit	35
Deflected Projectile Hit	15
Thrown or Detonated Object Hits an Enemy and Causes Damage	25
Force Attack Hit	15

SKILL POINTS AWARDED FOR FORCING AN ENEMY TO BLOCK

You can also earn skill points even if an opponent blocks your attack—however, you earn them at a reduced rate. Enhanced attacks cannot be blocked, so they are not included below.

Type of Attack	Skill Points Awarded
Light Attack Blocked	5
Strong Attack Blocked	10
Critical Attack Blocked	15
Deflected Projectile Blocked	5
Force Attack Blocked	10

LOSING SKILL POINTS

Now let's look at how you can lose skill points. The attacks against you can be either melee or projectile—the deduction is the same.

Action	Skill Points Lost
Hit By Light Attack	20
Hit By Enhanced Light Attack	30
Hit By Strong Attack	40
Hit By Enhanced Strong Attack	50
Hit By Hazard	40
Hit By Critical Attack	60
Hit By Enhanced Critical Attack	70
Hit By Deflected Projectile	30
Hit By Thrown or Detonated Object	50
Hit By Force Attack	30
Blocked Light Attack	10
Blocked Strong Attack	20
Blocked Critical Attack	30
Blocked Deflected Projectile	15
Blocked Force Attack	15

You also lose skill points for periods of time where you do not attack an enemy. The longer the period of time, the greater the drain on your skill meter.

Lapse of Time	Points Lost per Second
0–10 seconds	10
10–20 seconds	20
20–30 seconds	30
30+ seconds	40

Whenever you strike an enemy with your lightsaber—successfully or blocked—the loss of points instantly halts. It doesn't begin again until 10 seconds elapse without you hitting someone again.

You don't gain or lose points for missing with an attack or for hitting inanimate objects—destructible or not.

KILL RATINGS

Depending on how full the skill meter is when you kill an enemy, you receive a rating that determines how many experience points you earn. One of the following ratings appears after each kill.

Percentage of Skill Meter Full	Rating
0%–34%	Fair
35%–69%	Good
70%–99%	Impressive
100%	Masterful

When your skill meter fills completely, you gain the Masterful rating for your kills for 20 seconds, your lightsaber attacks do 150% of normal damage and enemies can't block your lightsaber attacks. At the end of this 20 seconds, your lightsaber attacks return to normal and your skill meter is reset to zero.

The Experience Meter

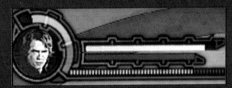

The experience meter shows how many experience points you have accumulated so far during a mission. The total length of the bar indicates the target number of experience points you can accumulate during the mission. Therefore, since missions have varying target numbers, the size of the bar varies based on the mission. Each segment of the meter represents 500 experience points. After you have completed a mission, you can then spend your experience points to upgrade your characters' abilities.

MUSTAFAR
HANGAR
ABC '04

GALLERY

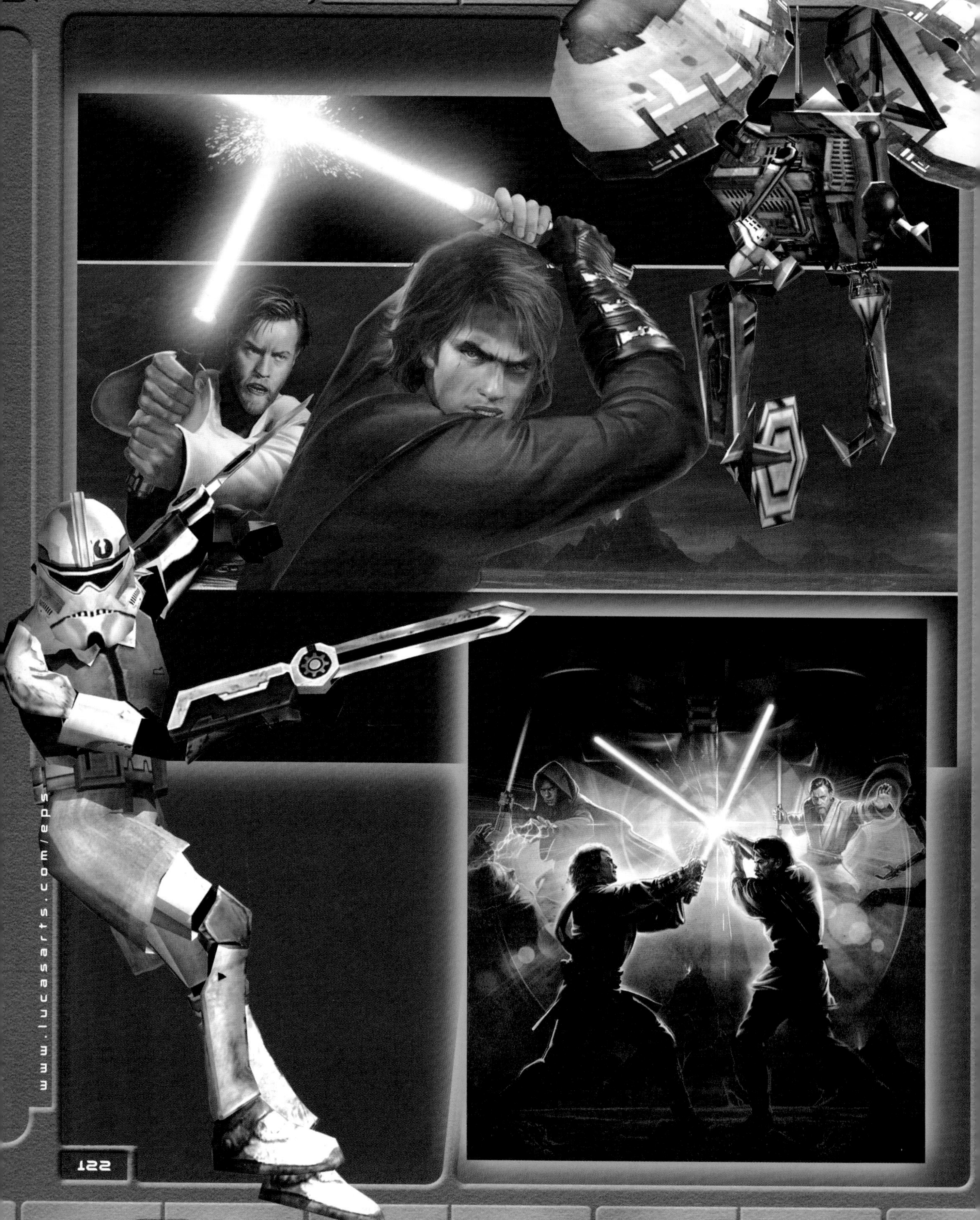

www.lucasarts.com/eps

Game Credits

STAR WARS: EPISODE III REVENGE OF THE SITH

Developed by The Collective

PROJECT EXECUTIVE STAFF
Creative Director, VP
Richard Hare

VP of Development
Gary Priest

VP of Production
Doug Hare

Technical Directors
Nathan Hunt
Feng "William" Chen

Animation Director
Mike Dietz

PROJECT LEADS
Producer
Cordy Rierson

Lead Artist
Dan Mycka

Lead Level Design
Antonio Barnes

Lead Combat Design & Scripting
Anthony Doe
David "Dr. Dave" Winstead

Lead Animator
Paul Belmore

Lead Character Artist
Kye-wan Sung

Lead Tools Programmer
Jason King

PRODUCTION
Assistant Producer
Jeremy Lee

Production Assistant
Brian Zenns

ART TEAM
Animation
Bryan Gillingham
Steven Hickcox
Douglas Pakidko

Characters
Peter Han
Allen Kerry

Visual Effects
Mark Bergo

Environment Art
David Robert Donatucci
Thomas Hamilton
Matt Olson
Bobby Rice
Jon Tucci

COMBAT DESIGN & SCRIPTING
Fredrick Corchero
Ryan W. Enslow
Parker Hamilton

LEVEL DESIGN
Jonathan Dumont
Lisa Hoffman
Rick Huenink
Daniel Jacobs
Carl Lavoie
Nick Parde
Temara Schulze

TOOLS AND TECHNOLOGY
Assistant Producer
Amy Kong

Core Gameplay Programming
Jason Boyle
David Mark Byttow

Core Technology
Kelly Brock
Justin Chin
Kevin Christensen
Randy Culley
Emil Dotchevski
Kevin Jenkins
Robert Slater
Eubank Wang

Tools Programmers
Zhenping Guo
Dustin McCartney
Mason McCuskey

SUPPORT STRUCTURE
VP, Chief Financial Officer
Steve Sardegna

System Administrator
Daniel Salzedo

Network Support Engineer
Erick Ocampo

Administrative
Shelley Campion

Human Resources
Karen Powers

ADDITIONAL SUPPORT
Additional Production
Rick Watters

Additional Scripting
Mark Acero

Additional Animation
Shawn Nelson

Additional Programming
Michel De Messieres
Jean-Louis Clement
Baback Elmieh
Ryan Greene
Vincent Scheib
George Sutty

Additional Storyboards
JJ Kirby

SPECIAL THANKS
To All Our Family and Friends

Published by LucasArts

PRODUCTION
Lead Producer
Isa Anne Stamos

Associate Producers
David Wehr
Justin Lambros
Matthew Fillbrandt

Assistant Producer
Corrine Wong

PRODUCTION LEADS
Technical Director
Cedric Bermond

Audio Lead
Ellen Meijers

Cutscenes Director
Adam Schnitzer

Lead Animator
Graham Annable

Lead Voice Editor
Harrison Deutsch

CUTSCENES
Animators
Armando Lluch
Joseph White
Mark Overney
Mike Dacko
Patrick Pryzbyla
Yu Hon Ng
Ryan Hood
Dave Bogan
Karin Nestor

Layout
Chris Weakley

Art Tech
Raven Alef

Storyboards / Concept Art
Amy Beth Christenson
Ian Berry

Avid Editor
Peter Whiteside

Writer
Jeremy Barlow

VISUAL EFFECTS
Eric Antanavich
Ryan Weiber

AUDIO
Sound Designer
Chris Hegstrom

Additional Sound Design
David Collins
Todd Davies
Julian Kwasneski

Music Editors
Mark Griskey
Jesse Harlin

Skywalker Sound

Cinematic Lead Sound Designer
Mac Smith

Games Sound Supervisor
Nick Peck
Cinematic Sound Designers
Brian Chumney
Aren Downie
Will Files
Al Nelson

Foley Artists
Ellen Heuer
Marnie Moore

Foley Mixer
Frank Aglieri-Rinella

Foley Recordist
George Peterson

Original *Star Wars* Sound effects
Ben Burtt

Original *Star Wars* music
Composed by John Williams.
(P) & (C) Lucasfilm Ltd. & TM.
All rights reserved. Used under
authorization.
Published by Bantha Music (BMI).
Administered and/or co-published
with Warner-Tamerlane Music
Publishing Corp.

Additional Music
Mark Griskey

CHARACTERS
Character Modelers
Mai Lea Nguyen
Barry McDougall

Associate Combat
Designer/Scripter
Andy Alamano

Character TD
Daryl Smolen
Peter Carisi-de Lappe

TECHNOLOGY
Audio Programming Support
Fred Mack
Paul Miller

Associate Art TD
Jonathan Tilden

LEVELS
Level Designers
Don Sielke
Ian Miller

Level Artists
James Michael Gutierrez
Nicholas Barnes
Robert Clarke

Combat Consultant and Special
Moves Choreographed by
Nick Gillard

TESTING
Senior Lead Tester
Chane Doc Hollander

Lead Tester
Johnny Szary

Assistant Lead Testers
Michael Blair
Patrick Bratton
James Morris

Testers
Ryan Adza
Seth Benton
Don Berger
Chris Chan
Henry Hall
Randy Ignacio
Chris Impola
Neilie Johnson
Ryan N. Jones
Clay Norman
Shinichiro Ohyama
Dan Reiley
Jonny Rice
Xavier Rodriguez
John Shields
Troy Sims
Dan Tambini
Chris Thomas
Michael Ward
Isaiah Webb
Jason Wick
Kevin Utschig
Jeff Yokomura
Zak Huntwork

Additional Testers
Eric Good
Mike Meeker
Edward Hyland
Jeff Husges

Senior Lead Compliance Tester
David Chapman

Lead Compliance Tester
Davey Lei

Compliance Testers
Sarah Cherlin
Chris Navarro
Nick Sinnott
QS Manager
Paul Purdy

QA Supervisor
Chuck McFadden

Product Support Supervisor
Jay Geraci

Hint Specialist
Tabitha Tosti

Mastering Lab Specialist
Wendy Kaplan

Mastering Technicians
Eric Rauch
Jay Tye
Scott Taylor

QS Coordinator
Kellie Walker

VOICE & INTERNATIONAL
Audio and International Manager
Darragh O'Farrell

Voice Directors
Darragh O'Farrell
Will Beckman
David Collins

Assistant Voice Director
Jennifer Sloan

Voice Editor
Cindy Wong

Assistant Voice Editor
G.W. Childs

International Localization Producer
Hiromi Okamoto

International Lead Tester/Production Assistant
Gary Chew

International Assistant Lead Tester
Ken Balough

International Testers
Dennis Bookout
Miguel Gonzalez
Jeremiah Lankford
Jeremy Leyland
Walker Richardson
Stephanie Taylor
Leif Youngquist
Greg Quinones

CAST
Mat Lucas
Anakin Skywalker

James Arnold Taylor
Obi-Wan Kenobi

Tom Kane
Yoda, Cin Drallig, Neimoidian Guard,
Neimoidian Brute, Jedi Leader,
Neimoidian Guard

Matthew Wood
General Grievous

TC Carson
Mace Windu

Andrew Chaikin
Clone Trooper, Clone Captain,
Commander Cody, Battledroid
Commander
Kari Wahlgren
Serra

Corey Burton
Count Dooku, Flying Battledroids,
Jedi Sniper, Rune Haako, Jedi
Brute, Jedi Pilot

Scott Lawrence
Darth Vader

Nick Jameson
Chancellor Palpatine, Darth Sidious,
Ben Kenobi, Neimoidian Aide,
Neimoidian Sniper

Scott Menville
Jedi Padawan

David W. Collins
BattleDroid, Wat Tambor,
Poggle The Lesser, Nute Gunray

Alethea McGrath
Jocasta Nu

Jarion Monroe
Grievous Bodyguard

MARKETING\PR\SALES

Product Marketing Manager
Sam Saliba

Senior Marketing Coordinator
Matt Shell

Marketing
John Geoghegen
Don Mesa

Public Relations
Anne Marie Stein
Jason Andersen
Hadley Fitzgerald

Sales and Channel Marketing
Mary Bihr
Meredith Cahill
Mike Maguire
Tim Moore
Greg Robles
Kristina Landies

Internet Marketing
Jim Passalacqua
Paul Warner

Additional Art
Robert Clarke
Marc Scott
Kye-wan Sung

Manual Writer
Matthew Keast

Manual Design
Patty Hill

ADDITIONAL SUPPORT

Consumer Insight
Sean Denny
Melissa Blegen

Content Supervisor
Ryan Kaufman

Lucas Licensing
Howard Roffman
Stacy Cheregotis
Chris Gollaher
Kristi Kaufman
Stacy Arnold

Lucas Digital
Paul Hill
Christy Castellano
Stephanie Hornish
Jerome Bakum
Lars Jensvold
Episode III Image Unit

Administrative Support
Peggy Ary
Mette Adams
Alison Gaiser

IT Support
Daryll Jacobson
Mike Etheridge
Jim Carpenter
Chad Williams

Business Affairs
Seth Steinberg
Mark Barbolak
John Garrett

Additional Design, Development and Management
Mike Gallo
Jon Knoles
Ian Milham
Daron Stinnett
Atsuko Matsumoto
Cory Allemeier
David Lee Swenson
Doug Modie
Eric Johnston
Greg Knight
J. White
John Howard
Karen Peterson
Malena Slettom
Matt Shores
Peter Hirschmann
Stephen McManus
Steven Chen
Kim Lyons
Martin Yee

SPECIAL THANKS
Jim Ward
Rick McCallum
Hayden Christensen
Ben Burtt
Denise Ream
Tippy Bushkin

Duncan Sinclair
Jim Tso
Chris Williams
Haden Blackman
Camela McLanahan
Matt White
Matthew Urban
Melissa Galicia
Mike Lampell
Mike Nelson
Colin Carley
The Chew & Ng Family
Corey Kapellas
Jeremy Louden
Erik O'Keady
Ken Rogers
Josh Lowden
Glenn Kiser
Matt Wood
Coya Elliott
Erik Foreman
Grace Aquino
Bill Stamos
Char & Lex Lambros
Helen Bermond
Wong/Lau Family
Jill Warren
Alec Roth
Sarah Esmaili
Michael Impola
Jennifer Luna
Gladys P. Thomas
Alyssa Sandoval
Haruka Oyama
"Moms" Norman
Gumbo Nick
Michele Forrest
Dana Clemens
Stacey Schrieber
Elizabeth Chapman-Reyna
The Reiley Family
Wo hen kuàilè Jia
Trisha Beltz
Peter Howard
The Chan Family
Kodiak Jack's
Jim Rice
Cricket
SBS
Seth Hollander & Family
Katy Walden

VERY SPECIAL THANKS
George Lucas

www.lucasarts.com/eps